# · TEN LATE ·
# BREAKFASTS

FOR
MARGARET SWEETNAM

ALEXANDRA CARLIER

# · TEN LATE ·
# BREAKFASTS

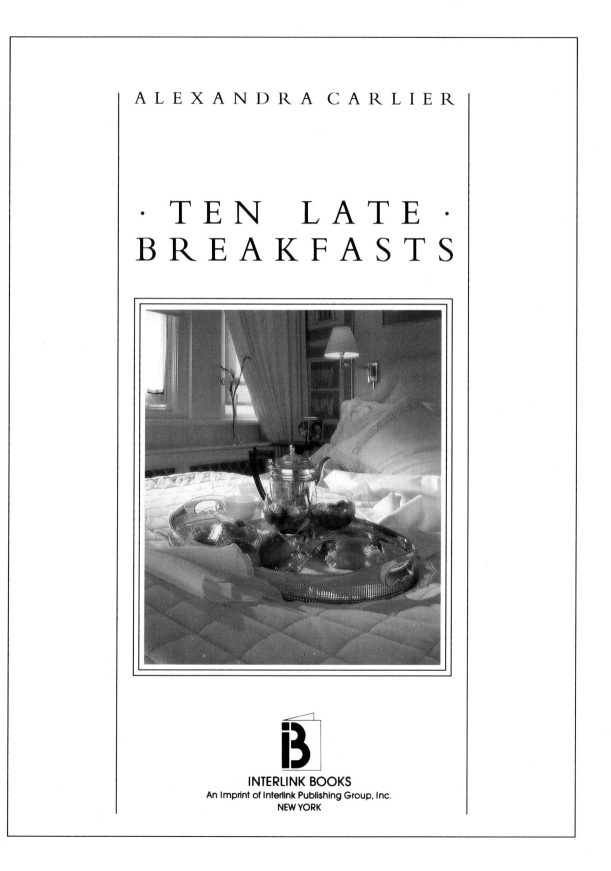

**INTERLINK BOOKS**
An Imprint of Interlink Publishing Group, Inc.
NEW YORK

First American edition published 1989 by
INTERLINK BOOKS
An imprint of Interlink Publishing Group, Inc.
99 Seventh Avenue
Brooklyn, New York 11215

Originally published in Great Britain by Ebury Press 1988

Designed and produced by
Sheldrake Press Ltd
188 Cavendish Road
London SW12 0DA

**Library of Congress Cataloging-in-Publication Data**

Carlier, Alexandra.
Ten late breakfasts / Alexandra Carlier.
    p.   cm.
    Includes index.
    ISBN 0-940793-24-5
    1. Breakfasts.  2. Menus.  I. Title.  II. Title: 10 late
breakfasts.
TX733.C37   1988                             88-21935
641.5′2—dc19                                      CIP

ISBN 0-940793-24-5

EDITOR: SIMON RIGGE
Managing Editor: Eleanor Lines
Art Direction and Book Design: Ivor Claydon, Bob Hook
Photography: Jan Baldwin assisted by Brian Leonard
Cover Photography: Bob Komar
Assistant Home Economist: Margaret Sweetnam
Stylist: Marie O'Hara
Artwork: James Robins
Assistant Editors: Tim Fraser, Vicky Hayward
Sub-Editor: Norma Macmillan
Editorial Assistant: Joan Lee

Printed in Hong Kong by Imago Publishing.

THE AUTHOR
Alexandra Carlier is a distinguished cookery writer and broadcaster. She
was a key contributor to the highly acclaimed Time-Life *Good Cook* series
and to the *Carrier's Kitchen* series published by Marshall Cavendish
(1981–83). She is the author of *The Dinner Party Book* (Collins, 1986), a
regular contributor to *Taste* magazine, and a guest cook for *The Times*.

# CONTENTS

# Introduction

I firmly believe that a well laden late breakfast table can provide a calming respite from hectic modern life. Too often breakfast is a hurried unsociable meal at an unspeakable hour. That is not the subject of this book. Here, you will find ideas and recipes for relaxed meals to enjoy with friends.

For many people, such late, leisurely breakfasts can only occur at the weekends or during holidays, which means they should be treated as a luxury to be savored in full. They can also be fun; the menus here are deliberately playful, drawing freely on historical precedents. There is no reason why we should not all enjoy the pleasures of the leisured classes in past centuries, when time and circumstances allow.

Hedonistic Roman statesmen certainly knew how to feast at breakfast; Clodius Albinus was reputed to have consumed up to a hundred tiny birds for his morning repast. In sixteenth-century England, breakfast may have been a simple affair for the dawn-rising laborers (bread or frumenty – a porridge of wheat and milk – and ale, consumed before heading off to work in the fields); but breakfast was not so simple for the gentry and nobility, certainly not for Queen Elizabeth I. As M. F. K. Fisher reports in *The Art of Eating*, 'the Queen, God be thanked, paid no attention to the new-style finicking, and made her first meal of the day light but sustaining: butter, bread (brown, to stay in the stomach longer and more wholesomely than white), a stew of mutton, a joint of beef, one of veal, some rabbits in a pie, chickens, and fruits, with beer and wine to wash all down in really hygienic fashion.' Even taking into account the fact that the Queen rose early, she can hardly have suffered hunger pangs between breakfast and the main meal of the day which was served at 11 am.

By the seventeenth century, breakfast in England had become a more modest affair. The 'new-style finicking,' the trends from Italy and elsewhere in Europe toward a lighter style of eating, were making their mark. People leading a town life tended to pass breakfast over, unless they were entertaining. On January 1, 1661, when Samuel Pepys entertained brother Thomas, father Dr. Thomas Pepys and uncle Fenner and his two sons to breakfast, he noted in his diary: 'And I have for them a barrel of oysters, a dish of neat's tongues, and a dish of Anchoves – wine of all sorts and Northdown ale. We were very merry till about 11 a-clock, and then they went away.'

Pepys does not mention coffee, which had established itself as a breakfast drink in England by the mid to late 1650s. It had first been popularized in Europe by a Turkish ambassador at the court of Louis XIV and probably made its appearance in England during Cromwell's protectorate. Perhaps Pepys disliked the taste, or perhaps he paid attention to the many warnings from medical and clerical circles that it was bad for health and soul.

Similar criticisms were later leveled at tea, which Pepys would not have drunk by 1661; tea is thought to have been introduced into England from Asia by Lord Arlington in 1666, but it took a further thirty years or so to become a firmly established breakfast beverage. The ladies of the period were generally keener to move toward non-alcoholic drinks, including tea and coffee, than their menfolk, who clung to the old customs of wine, ale or spirits for as long as they could.

By the eighteenth century, tea and coffee had become cheaper, and the dinner hour had moved beyond noon. These two factors conspired to make breakfast, as we generally know it now, universal in England. For the middle and upper classes, there would be a good selection of cold dishes, as well as a hot dish and an array of breads, butter and preserves.

Meanwhile, in America, specifically New Orleans, we witness the birth of the American brunch, a meal combining breakfast and lunch. Opinion is divided as to how and why it was born. One school of thought is that the French merchants, who were up well before dawn with no time or inclination for eating, decided to meet in town and take a civilized breakfast when work was finished in the late morning. A second theory is that after the first Christmas mass in 1718 the settlers held a celebratory, and highly social, late breakfast, and the event became a habit.

By the end of the following century the new meal had crossed the Atlantic: in 1896 London's *Punch* magazine wrote, 'To be fashionable nowadays we must "brunch;" ' and four years later *The Westminster Gazette* quipped:

'Perish scrambling breakfast, formal lunch,
Hardened nightbirds fondly cherish
All the subtle charms of brunch.'

However, most people in nineteenth-century America and England continued to breakfast early and briskly. Many Victorians, having moved to the newly built suburbs, had to leave earlier for work in order to commute to the growing commercial centers in the cities. For the poor, the food would probably have been no more than a piece of bread. For others, it was leftover cold meat or fresh eggs, fruit and beverages.

Of course, for some Victorians, breakfast was a grander, more leisurely affair. The rich empire-builders and landowners enjoyed entertaining and had the resources to do so on a grand scale. There were abundant servants and plentiful food, as one would expect of an imperial race. When house parties were in full swing, it was not uncommon for breakfast to be available from 8 am to 2 pm. A large sideboard groaned with food, and butlers and maids were at hand to fetch, carry and replenish. These lavish repasts were responsible for the reputation of the Great British Breakfast. Later, the Edwardians continued the tradition and, with improved refrigerated transport, were able to serve a greater variety of imported tropical fruit. Nowadays, the Great British Breakfast is something of a rarity.

The twentieth century has also brought developments to the breakfast table. Thanks to the United States, fruit has become an almost indispensable adjunct to breakfast, and we can enjoy a range of wonderfully innovative egg dishes such as Eggs Benedict. While the British upper classes were turning breakfast into a banquet, Dr. Max Bircher-Benner in Switzerland was formulating his recipe for muesli. Faced with a patient unable to digest cooked food, a colleague jokingly suggested that Bircher-Benner try Pythagoras's fifth-century B.C. treatment of mashed raw fruit, honey and goat's milk. The somewhat sceptical Bircher-Benner tried Pythagoras's cure, the patient recovered and now millions of people start the day with a bowl of raw grains, seeds, nuts and fruit.

A glance at hotel and restaurant menus throughout the world would suggest that the American breakfast has made greater impact on this century than any other. True, I'm excluding the so-called 'continental breakfast;' this is because too many hotels and homes, even in France, abuse the term by serving a cold, poor-quality, virtually butterless croissant or roll with an indifferent jam, nondescript coffee with cold milk or a poor-quality tea – and a bag at that! Orange juice, usually said to be fresh, more often than not has a lingering taste of the can from whence it came.

Today, most people have a hurried, early breakfast forced upon them five days of the week. But that still leaves two days to live freely, to rise late if one wishes and to be one's own person. These times, when creative thoughts can take shape, are complemented perfectly by the late breakfast, which can begin somewhere between late morning and noon or even later.

# BREADS

For many people, bread is an essential part of breakfast. And home-made bread is almost always better than anything you can buy. Yet, as Eliza Acton wrote in *The English Bread Book*, published in 1857, 'A very exaggerated idea of the difficulty and trouble of bread-making prevails amongst people who are entirely ignorant of the process.' In fact, much of the work in yeast cookery is done, not by the cook, but by the dough itself. After the cook has mixed the ingredients and kneaded the dough, the yeast sets to work, gradually producing carbon dioxide from the moistened flour. This fermentation gently expands the dough to create a light, airy loaf.

Not all breads depend on yeast to raise them. Some, such as Quick White Soda Bread and Quick Cornbread Rolls, are raised by baking soda or powder. These breads are ideal if you are in a hurry; they rise only in the oven and must be baked as soon as they are prepared.

## BASIC BROWN ROLLS AND LOAVES

### INGREDIENTS

| |
| --- |
| *1 tbsp sugar* |
| *scant 2 cups lukewarm water* |
| *1 tbsp active dry yeast* |
| *2¼ cups + 2 tbsp white bread flour* |
| *3 cups whole wheat flour* |
| *1 tbsp salt* |
| *1 tbsp olive or sunflower oil* |

### TO FINISH (OPTIONAL)

| |
| --- |
| *3–4 tbsp cracked wheat or poppy, sunflower or sesame seeds, or a mixture of these* |

**Makes about 20 rolls, or 2 large loaves, or 3 small ones**

This recipe makes an excellent all-purpose bread. The mixture of white and wholemeal flours yields a delicious loaf with the nutty flavor of the germ and husk, with some of the lightness of white bread. It is very good toasted.

Dissolve the sugar in the water. Add the yeast and whisk lightly. Cover and leave in a warm place for about 15 minutes, or until the mixture starts to foam. Meanwhile, sift the flours and the salt into a large mixing bowl; tip in the bran left in the sieve. Put in a very low oven for about 8 minutes.

Make a well in the flour and add the yeast mixture and oil. Gradually mix to form a dough. Turn out on to a well-floured surface and knead for 10 minutes or until elastic and no longer sticky. Add a little more flour if necessary. Return the dough to a clean, dry bowl, cover with plastic wrap and leave in a warm place to rise for 1½ hours or until doubled in volume. (The dough is ready when a finger pressed into it leaves a dent.)

Punch down the dough and knead it again briefly on a floured surface. For rolls, cut the dough into small pieces and stamp each piece with a clenched fist, to expel air. After shaping, place the rolls on a greased or floured baking sheet.

*For classic rolls:* shape the pieces into balls, then slash the tops with a shallow cross; this creates a wider area of softer crust.

*For cigar rolls:* form fat cigar shapes and cut a single shallow slash along the top of each.

*For knots:* roll the dough pieces into rope shapes and tie each into a knot.

*For cloverleaf rolls:* shape small balls about 1 inch in diameter and join them in clusters of three to make a cloverleaf shape.

*For a cob loaf:* mold the dough into two large balls and slash the tops into a shallow cross or into a complex checkerboard design. Place on a greased baking sheet.

*For a standard loaf:* form the dough into one or two cylinders and transfer to well-greased loaf pans. Make a slash along the top.

Cover the dough with a damp cloth and leave to rise in a warm place, rolls for about 25 minutes and loaves for 50 minutes.

Preheat the oven to 425°.

If you like, sprinkle the dough with cracked wheat or seeds.

Bake rolls for about 20 minutes, then turn them upside down and bake for a further 3 to 4 minutes to brown and crisp the bottoms. Bake cob loaves for 40 to 50 minutes. Bake standard loaves for about 30 minutes, then remove them from their pans and bake for a further 10 minutes or so on a baking sheet to crisp the sides and bottoms.

Test if the loaves are done by rapping on the base; they should sound hollow.

Cool on a wire rack.

## QUICK WHITE SODA BREAD

### INGREDIENTS

| |
|---|
| 3 cups + 3 tbsp all-purpose flour |
| 1 tsp salt |
| 1 tsp baking soda |
| about 1¼ cups buttermilk or plain yogurt |

**Makes an 8-inch round loaf or 2 very small loaves**

There is no need to wake at dawn to bake fresh bread for breakfast. Breads, such as this one, leavened with baking soda, need no rising time. When moistened, the soda produces carbon dioxide that expands in the hot oven to raise the loaf. Within an hour of mixing the dough the bread is ready for the table. The result is a bread with a crumblier texture than that of yeast bread.

For Quick Brown Soda Bread replace the entire quantity of white flour with whole wheat flour. For a lighter brown loaf, replace only half the quantity of white flour with whole wheat flour.

Preheat the oven to 425°. Sift the flour, salt and soda into a large bowl. Add the buttermilk or yogurt and mix to a dough, incorporating 1 to 2 tablespoons of warm water if the dough is stiff.

Turn the dough on to a floured surface and knead it briefly and lightly for no more than 3 minutes. Form into a single round loaf or two smaller ones, then score a deep cross on the top to make four quarters. Transfer the loaf to a floured baking sheet and cover with a deep cake pan. Alternatively, place the dough inside an oiled, warmed, heavy pot, preferably made of cast iron. The base of the pot should be a few inches larger all around than the dough. Cover with a lid.

Bake the bread for 30 minutes. Remove the cake pan or pot lid and bake for a further 10 minutes or until the crust is golden brown. Cool the loaf on a wire rack, then break it into four wedges and slice it.

## QUICK CORNBREAD ROLLS

### INGREDIENTS

| |
|---|
| 1 cup yellow cornmeal |
| ½ cup whole wheat flour |
| ½ tsp salt |
| 1½ tsp baking powder |
| 1 large egg |
| 1 tbsp light brown sugar |
| ⅔ cup milk |
| 1 tbsp sunflower or olive oil |

**Makes 6 to 9**

Cornmeal, ground from maize, has a slightly sweet flavor. Use yellow, rather than white, cornmeal to color these rolls delicately.

Have ready a nonstick muffin pan. In the absence of a nonstick variety, line the pan with greased nonstick baking parchment paper. Preheat the oven to 400°.

Sift the cornmeal, flour, salt and baking powder into a large mixing bowl and add the bran left in the sieve. In a separate bowl, beat the egg, then add the sugar, milk and oil, beating with a whisk until thoroughly blended. Make a well in the flour mixture and gradually add the egg and milk mixture, beating to form a smooth batter. Spoon the batter into the prepared pan.

Bake for about 20 minutes, or until the rolls are golden brown and risen. Cool on a wire rack before serving.

## SAFFRON AND HERB BREAD

### INGREDIENTS

| |
|---|
| 1 tbsp sugar |
| 3 tbsp lukewarm water |
| 1 tbsp active dry yeast |
| about 5 cups white bread flour, sifted |
| 1 tsp salt |
| about 1 cup lukewarm milk |
| 3 large eggs |
| scant ½ tsp powdered saffron dissolved in 2 tbsp hot water |
| 2 sticks unsalted butter, softened and broken into small bits |
| 2 tbsp finely chopped fresh marjoram |
| 2 tbsp finely chopped fresh oregano |
| 1 tbsp finely chopped fresh parsley |
| 1 egg yolk mixed with 2 tbsp water, for the glaze |

**Makes 1 large loaf**

There is simply no commercial equivalent to this savory bread. Like all yeast breads it takes time – but for most of this time the dough is rising or baking on its own – and the result is superb. The saffron, made from the dried stamens of a type of crocus, not only colors the bread a bright yellow, it also lends a unique spicy flavor.

In a small bowl, dissolve the sugar in the water. Add the yeast and whisk. Set the yeast mixture aside in a warm place for about 15 minutes or until the mixture foams slightly.

Pour the yeast mixture into a large bowl. Whisk in one-third of the sifted flour, the salt and the milk to make a thick batter. Cover the bowl with plastic wrap and leave to rise in a warm place for about 1 hour, or until doubled in volume.

Whisk in the eggs and the saffron. Whisk in the softened butter a few bits at a time, then stir in the remaining sifted flour a handful at a time, alternating with the herbs. Blend the mixture by hand to form a loose, sticky dough.

Turn out the dough on to a well-floured surface. Knead for 10 to 15 minutes, or until the dough is smooth and elastic. Return the dough to a clean, dry bowl, cover with plastic wrap and leave to rise in a warm place for 1½ to 2 hours or until tripled in volume.

Punch down the dough and shape it into a loaf – it looks particularly attractive formed into a ring. To do this, shape the dough into a round, then press your fingers into the middle and gradually stretch the dough outward to form a ring. If the dough resists being stretched, rest it for 10 minutes, covered, then continue. Place the shaped dough on a greased baking sheet. Cover with a cloth and leave to rise in a warm place for about 1 hour.

Preheat the oven to 400°. Brush the dough with the egg yolk, glaze and bake for about 45 minutes or until the bread sounds hollow when rapped on the base.

If necessary, cover the surface loosely with foil to prevent over-browning toward the end of cooking. Remove the loaf from the oven and cool on a wire rack before cutting.

# QUICK BRAN AND RAISIN MUFFINS

## INGREDIENTS

| |
|---|
| 1⅓ cups white bread flour |
| 1 tsp salt |
| 1 tsp baking soda |
| 1⅔ cups bran |
| ¼ cup raisins |
| 1¾ cups milk |
| ¼ cup liquid honey |
| 3 tbsp sunflower oil or melted clarified butter |
| ½ tsp ground cinnamon |

**Makes 6 to 8**

You don't have to be a devotee of bran to enjoy these muffins. I like them best freshly baked, still warm from the oven, with cold unsalted butter and lavender honey.

Preheat the oven to 350°. Sift the flour, salt and soda into a large mixing bowl. Stir in the bran and raisins. Make a well in the center and add the milk, honey and oil or butter. Gradually draw the dry ingredients into the center to form a soft batter. Stir in the cinnamon.

Transfer the batter to an oiled muffin pan and bake for about 30 minutes, or until the muffins are risen and pulling away from the sides of the pan. Cool on a wire rack. Serve warm or cold, or reheated in the oven. These muf-

fins keep extremely well in an airtight container.

# PARSLEY BREAD

## INGREDIENTS

| |
|---|
| 2 tsp active dry yeast |
| about 3 cups lukewarm milk |
| 8 cups white bread flour |
| 2 tsp salt |
| 6 tbsp unsalted butter, softened and broken into small bits |
| ⅓ cup finely chopped fresh parsley |

**Makes 2 large loaves**

This lightly enriched bread, prettily flecked with green, goes very well with egg and meat dishes.

Dissolve the yeast in the milk, whisk it lightly, and set aside until it foams slightly – about 15 minutes.

Sift the flour and salt into a bowl. Add the yeast mixture and the softened butter and mix with your hands to form a sticky dough. Turn the dough on to a floured surface and knead vigorously, gradually incorporating the parsley. Continue to knead for 10 to 15 minutes, adding a little more flour if necessary, to form a fairly firm, smooth dough. Leave the dough to rise in a large bowl, covered with plastic wrap, until doubled in bulk – 1½ to 2 hours.

Knead the dough again and divide it into six balls. Roll each ball into a strand. Take three strands and braid them together; do the same with the other three strands. Transfer the braids to greased baking sheets. Cover with a damp cloth and leave in a warm place to rise until doubled in bulk – 45 to 60 minutes.

Preheat the oven to 450°.

Bake the bread for 40 to 45 minutes or until it sounds hollow when you rap the base with your knuckles. Cool on wire racks.

## THREE-SEED LOAF

### INGREDIENTS

| |
|---|
| 1 tbsp active dry yeast |
| about 2 cups lukewarm water |
| 2⅓ cups white bread flour, warmed |
| 2 cups whole wheat flour, warmed |
| 1 cup rye flour, warmed |
| 1 tbsp salt |
| 1 tsp sugar |
| 3 tbsp sesame seeds |
| ⅓ cup sunflower seeds |
| 3 tbsp poppy seeds |

### FOR THE CRUST

| |
|---|
| 1 tbsp each sesame, sunflower and poppy seeds |

**Makes 1 large loaf**

Here's an example of beginner's luck. Bored with store-bought bread I decided to make my own. I mixed three types of flour, added three types of seed, and the result was delicious. Of course, if you cannot find rye flour, replace it with more of the other two.

Mix the yeast with one-third of the water, whisk and leave in a warm place for about 15 minutes, or until the mixture foams slightly.

Sift the warmed flours and salt into a large bowl, and add the bran left in the sieve. Stir in the sugar and the seeds. Add the yeast mixture and the remaining water and mix to a dough. Knead for 10 minutes or until elastic and no longer sticky. Transfer to a clean, dry bowl, cover with plastic wrap and leave to rise in a warm place for 2 hours.

Punch down the dough and knead it again briefly. Divide the dough in half, then join it up again, shaping it into a rectangular loaf that is folded into a neat pleat along the top, thus making a ridge that will form a thick crust. Distribute the seeds for the crust on a very lightly floured board, and roll the entire loaf lightly over this. Place in a large, oiled loaf pan. Make three diagonal slashes along the top of the loaf, and add more seeds to this top crust if you like. Cover the loaf with a cloth and leave to rise in a warm place for 30 minutes.

Preheat the oven to 425°. Put a roasting pan filled with cold water on the bottom shelf of the oven to form a steam tray. Bake the bread for 40 minutes, then transfer it to a baking sheet and continue to bake for a further 10 minutes to color the sides. Transfer to a wire rack to cool.

## ENGLISH MUFFINS

### INGREDIENTS

| |
|---|
| 3¼ cups white bread flour |
| 1⅔ cups all-purpose flour |
| 1 tsp salt |
| 1 tsp sugar |
| 1 small package quick-rise yeast |
| 2½ cups lukewarm milk |
| small amount of rice flour, cornstarch or all-purpose flour |
| about 3 tbsp sunflower oil or melted lard |

**Makes 14 to 18**

There is no consensus on how to serve muffins; the choice is yours. Many people split them and toast them, while others merely split them, butter and eat. However, it has also been argued that the only way to serve muffins is to open them up slightly, then to toast them back and front before tearing them open and spreading with butter.

Sift the two types of flour, the salt, sugar and yeast into a large bowl. Mix well and transfer to a very low oven to warm through for about 8 minutes.

Make a well in the middle of the flour mixture and gradually incorporate the milk, mixing with a wooden spoon. Cover with plastic wrap and leave in a warm place to rise for about 50 minutes; during this time the dough should double in bulk.

Turn out the dough on to a surface dusted preferably with rice flour; otherwise, use cornstarch or flour. Dust your hands with rice flour – or the alternatives – and form the dough into 14 to 18 equal rounds. Dust a baking sheet or wooden board with rice flour and transfer the rounds to it. Cover with a cloth and leave in a warm place to rise for about 40 minutes or until doubled in volume.

Heat a griddle. Brush it with oil and cook the muffins in batches over a low to medium heat for 10 to 15 minutes on each side or until golden brown. Keep the batches warm in a cloth or low oven, or cool on a wire rack before toasting to serve.

## CRUMPETS
### INGREDIENTS

| |
|---|
| about 5 cups white bread flour |
| 1½ tsp salt |
| 1 small package quick-rise yeast |
| 5 tbsp skim milk powder |
| 2½ cups lukewarm water |
| 1½ tsp baking soda mixed with about ⅞ cup lukewarm water |

**Makes about 20**

You can serve these English favorites warm, fresh off the griddle, although it is generally thought preferable to serve them toasted. Always accompany with plenty of butter and, if you like, fruit preserves.

Sift the flour and salt into a large bowl. Stir in the yeast and warm in a very low oven for about 4 minutes. Remove the bowl from the oven and add the milk powder. Make a well in the center of the dry ingredients and gradually mix in enough of the water to form a stiff batter. Beat well for about 5 minutes. Cover with plastic wrap and set aside in a warm place to rise for about 1 hour.

Add the soda and water mixture to the batter, and beat until smooth. The batter should be runny so add a little more lukewarm water if necessary. Leave the batter to rest, covered, for 30 minutes or until frothy.

When the batter is ready, grease some crumpet rings and the griddle with lard. Position the rings on the griddle, and place over medium to high heat. Half-fill the rings with batter and cook for about 4 minutes or until the surface of each crumpet is firm and springy. Turn them over and cook for a further 1 to 2 minutes.

Remove the crumpets from the rings and wrap them in a cloth to keep them warm while you cook the rest of the batter.

For other bread recipes see Oatcakes (page 42), Bagels (page 63), *Pain aux Fruits Secs* (page 98), Blueberry Muffins (page 64) and Blini (page 61).

*Selection of Breads, Rolls and Muffins*

# E G G S

Eggs, one of the most versatile of breakfast foods, appear on the breakfast table in many forms: boiled, coddled, poached, scrambled, fried or beaten in an omelette. They are even eaten raw for breakfast as part of that supposed hangover cure, the Prairie Oyster (page 20). Whenever possible, buy free-range eggs; they have far more flavor than the battery variety.

*Boiled Eggs*
The eggs should be lowered into gently simmering water, and their cooking time judged from this instant. Cooking times are as follows:

|  | Extra-large or large eggs | Smaller eggs |
|---|---|---|
| Very soft cooked | 3½ to 4 minutes | 2½ to 3 minutes |
| Soft yolk and hard white | 4½ minutes | 3½ minutes |
| Hard-cooked | 8 minutes | 6 minutes |

New-laid eggs will take up to a minute longer than these times.

Eggs taken straight from the refrigerator will take 1 to 2 minutes longer to cook than those at room temperature. It is not advisable to boil refrigerated eggs, but if you do, place a metal teaspoon in the pan to help prevent the shell from cracking with the shock of temperature change.

*Eggs in a Coddler*
Lightly butter a porcelain coddler. Break 1 or 2 eggs into it (depending on the size of the coddler). Top with a little salt and freshly ground pepper, a scrap of butter and, if you wish, a little cream. Screw on the top of the coddler and immerse it to seven-eighths of its depth in a pan of gently simmering water. Cook for 10 minutes.

*Fried Eggs, Sunny Side Up*
Melt enough butter in a heavy frying pan to cover the bottom generously, adding a little olive oil to prevent burning. Alternatively, you can use oil alone, or bacon fat instead of butter. (Fat is not necessary if you use a nonstick pan, but the flavor of the eggs will, of course, be different.)

Heat the pan over medium heat. Do not add the eggs until the fat in the pan is hot. When it is, you can break the eggs directly into the pan, or you can break them first, one at a time, into a cup. The latter method enables you to rescue the situation if the yolk should break.

Tilt the pan, collect some fat on a spoon and baste the eggs with the fat. Cover the pan with a lid. After about 1 minute the whites should be set and the yolks secure. Season with salt and pepper. Transfer to a warm plate and serve immediately.

*Fried Eggs, Over Easy*
Prepare the pan and add the eggs as for Fried Eggs, Sunny Side Up. Once the eggs are in the pan, baste the yolks with a little of their setting white; this will protect the yolk when the egg is turned over. Count about 1 minute, during which time the underside will set, then turn the eggs over using a slotted spatula or slice. (If you are frying only one egg, you can toss it over.) Cook for ½ to 1 minute on the other side, and add seasoning. Slide on to a warmed plate, and serve at once.

*Poached Eggs*
A lot of old wives' tales have been written about the poaching of eggs. Myths, along the lines that a pinch of salt or a drop of vinegar added to the poaching water makes all the difference, continue to prevail. The facts concerning success are as follows.

Use only very fresh eggs, otherwise the whites will be very thin, stringy and apt to spread.

Bring a wide, shallow pan of water to simmering point. Crack the eggs directly into the water, if you wish. However, I find it easier to break each egg into a cup and dip the base of the cup briefly into the water to coagulate the white, just a little, before slipping the egg into the gently simmering water. Poach no more than four eggs at a time, and cover the pan with a lid during cooking. Remove each egg, using a slotted spoon, after about 3 minutes of cooking and transfer to a cloth to drain. Trim away any ragged edges before serving.

If the egg is to be kept warm briefly, transfer it to a bowl of warm – not hot – water. Alternatively, if you wish to arrest the cooking of the egg, so that it can be used in a dish such as Eggs Florentine, then you should immerse the egg in cold water.

*Poached Eggs with Herbs and Butter*
Poach the eggs lightly and arrest the cooking by dipping them in cold water. Drain well, then sauté very gently for a few minutes in melted unsalted butter with chopped fresh herbs – about ½ tablespoon for each egg. Fresh tarragon is particularly good with eggs, although

marjoram, parsley and chives are also possibilities. Add a squeeze of lemon juice just before serving.

For other poached egg dishes see Eggs Benedict (page 59) and Eggs Florentine (page 49).

*Scrambled Eggs*
Everyone has their favorite way of scrambling eggs. This is mine.

Butter the upper pan or bowl of a *bain-marie* or double boiler. Bring some water to simmering point in the lower pan. Lightly beat (don't overbeat) the eggs in a bowl. Season, and add just under 2 tablespoons unsalted butter, very finely diced, for every four eggs. Tip the mixture into the top of the *bain-marie* and set it over the simmering water.

Cook, stirring continuously with a wooden spoon, using a figure-eight movement, until the eggs are soft and creamy. Remove from the heat. Should you wish to arrest the cooking, immerse the base of the cooking vessel in cold or iced water.

When the scrambled eggs begin to thicken, you may add any of the following:
finely chopped fresh herbs such as marjoram, tarragon or parsley;
smoked salmon, cut into small slivers, plus chopped fresh parsley;
finnan haddie, cooked and flaked;
croûtons fried in butter;
sliced mushrooms turned gently in a little butter, with chopped fresh or dried thyme;
chicken livers, lightly sautéed in a little butter until just pink, then sliced;
veal or lamb's kidney, cut up and lightly sautéed in butter until just pink.

*Omelettes*
The highly versatile omelette can be any size or shape, with or without a filling. As a general rule, a 7-inch pan holds an omelette made from two large eggs. This is usually large enough for most people at breakfast, but the hungry may wish to use three eggs, and a slightly larger pan.

The basic guidelines for cooking an omelette are as follows.

Break the eggs into a shallow dish. Add about 1 tablespoon cold unsalted butter, cut into small dice, for every two eggs used. Heat an omelette pan, adding a small nut of butter to it. While the nut of butter melts, beat the eggs lightly with a fork. When the butter in the pan starts to foam, tip in the egg mixture. Tilt the pan and pass the flat of a fork through the mixture so that any uncooked egg can make contact with the hot pan. When set on the base but still creamy on top, add any filling that you may wish to employ (see the variations above). Roll up the omelette, seal its edges against the side of the pan and tip on to a warm plate.

For an Oyster Omelette, see page 60.

# SPICY SCRAMBLED EGGS

## INGREDIENTS

| |
|---|
| 1 onion, finely chopped |
| 3½ tbsp olive oil or melted clarified butter |
| 1 large tomato, peeled, seeded and chopped |
| ⅛ tsp hot chili powder |
| 1 tbsp finely chopped fresh ginger root |
| ¼ tsp turmeric |
| 6 extra large eggs |
| salt and freshly ground pepper |
| 1½ tbsp finely chopped fresh coriander (cilantro) |

**Serves 2 to 3**

The flavorings for this dish are borrowed from India. They were popular spices in Victorian England.

Sweat the onion very gently in the oil or butter, using a fairly wide heavy sauté pan with the lid on; this will take about 20 minutes. Stir in the tomato, chili powder, ginger and turmeric, then cook for a further few minutes to soften the tomato.

Beat the eggs lightly with a fork and season them. Add them to the pan and cook over very low heat, stirring continuously with a wooden spoon using a figure-eight movement, until the mixture is soft and creamy. Toward the end of cooking, stir in 1 tablespoon of the chopped coriander.

You can serve the eggs by themselves or on toast or bread of some kind. Scatter the remaining coriander over the eggs as a garnish.

For other scrambled egg dishes see Oeufs à l'Amour (page 122) and Scrambled Eggs in Smoked Salmon Packages (page 123).

# PRESERVES

Home-made, fruit-laden jams, jellies and marmalades are a welcome addition to any breakfast table. There is no mystery to making your own preserves. The three essential ingredients are fruit, water and sugar. The sugar preserves the fruit and, with the pectin and acid from the fruit, ensures that the mixture sets. Once the hot preserve has reached its setting point, ladle it into jars. When cooled, put them away in a cool, dark, dry cupboard. Stored this way preserves retain their flavor and bright color for at least a year.

## TO TEST FOR SETTING

*Using a thermometer*
Use a sugar thermometer with a clip, so that you can fasten it to the inside of the pan. Warm the thermometer in hot water before putting it into the simmering preserve. Cook the preserve until the thermometer registers 220–221°.

*Using a chilled plate*
Spoon a little boiling jam on to a well-chilled plate or saucer. Allow it to cool for a few minutes. If the jam has reached setting point, a skin will form, which will wrinkle when pushed with your fingertip. If the sample jam remains fluid, continue boiling the jam and test again after a few minutes.

## PERFECT POTTING

*To sterilize jars*
The easiest way is to wash them along with lids and any fittings, in a dishwasher set on high heat. If you are devoid of dishwasher, wash and rinse the jars thoroughly, then put them in a large pan. Add enough water to immerse the jars, then boil them for 5 minutes. When you are almost ready to use the jars, invert them on to clean dry towels to drain. If the jars become cold, warm them – so as to prevent cracking when filled with hot jam – in an oven set at 275°.

*To cover and seal*
Fill each warm, sterilized jar to within about ½-inch of its rim with hot preserve. Because mold and other spoilage can occur in preserves, especially if stored at temperatures over 50°, it is a good idea to finish them with a short processing in a boiling water bath. To do this, cover the filled jars (which must be able to withstand the high water temperature without breaking), place them on a rack in a large deep pan and pour over boiling water to cover the jars by 1 to 2 inches. Bring the water back to a full boil and boil for 10 minutes.

Remove the jars, complete the seals if necessary and leave to cool before labeling and storing.

With this marmalade, the grapefruit flesh is discarded once squeezed of its juice. The result is a fairly clear marmalade in which the peel is suspended. It is also rather tart, so add up to 1 cup more sugar if you have a sweetish tooth. For an orange marmalade see Chunky Marmalade with Whisky (page 43).

Cut the grapefruit in half and squeeze out the juice. Strain it. Reserve the juice and the seeds; tie the seeds in a cheesecloth bag. Remove and discard the membrane and white pith from the grapefruit, then slice the peel finely. Soak the peel with the bag of seeds overnight in the fruit juice and the water.

The following day, simmer the ingredients in a large pan for about 1 hour or until the peel has softened. Remove and discard the bag of seeds. Over very low heat, or off the heat, add the sugar and stir until it is dissolved. Over high heat, boil hard for about 30 minutes or until setting point is reached. Ladle into warm sterilized jars. After about 10 minutes, stir to distribute the peel evenly, then cover. Process if liked, seal and label.

## CLASSIC GRAPEFRUIT MARMALADE

### INGREDIENTS

| |
|---|
| *3 lb grapefruit* |
| *about 4 qt water* |
| *4½ lb (9 cups) sugar* |

**Makes about 8 pounds**

## PRESERVE OF GRAPEFRUIT AND LIME FANS

### INGREDIENTS

*3 lb grapefruit, preferably a mixture of pink and yellow*

*6 limes*

*4½ qt water*

*5¼ lb (10½ cups) sugar*

**Makes about 9 pounds**

For this preserve, I cut whole fruit – flesh and peel – into fan shapes. The fans look particularly colorful and pretty when both pink and yellow grapefruit are used with the limes.

Cut the grapefruit in half. Remove the seeds, wrap them in cheesecloth and set aside. Cut the grapefruit halves in half. Starting at the wide, fleshy end of each quarter section, slice the grapefruit thinly, discarding the thick pith and peel when you reach it. Cut the quarter slices of flesh in half to make fan shapes; set aside. Cut the limes into similar fan shapes. Soak the fruit with the bag of seeds overnight in the water.

The following day, simmer the ingredients together in a large pan for 30 to 40 minutes or until soft. Remove and discard the bag of seeds. Over very low heat, or off the heat, add the sugar and stir until it is dissolved completely. Over high heat, bring to the boil and boil hard for about 30 minutes or until setting point is reached. Ladle into warm, sterilized jars. After about 10 minutes, stir each jar to distribute the fruit, then cover. Process if liked, seal and label.

## PLUM AND ORANGE PRESERVE

### INGREDIENTS

*3 lb firm plums, stalks removed*

*2 thin-skinned oranges*

*1½ cups water*

*3 lb (6 cups) sugar*

**Makes about 5 pounds**

To give this preserve a distinctive almond-like flavor, extract the kernels from about a dozen plum pits, then wrap them in cheesecloth and include them in the pan. Remove the kernels before potting the jam.

Quarter and pit the plums. Place the fruit in a large pan. Finely pare the zest from the oranges and chop it finely. Squeeze the juice from the oranges; there should be about 1 cup. Add the zest and juice and the water to the pan. Simmer for about 45 minutes or until the plums are tender.

Remove the pan from the heat. Add the sugar and stir until dissolved, then return to a high heat and boil hard for 20 to 30 minutes or until setting point is reached. Ladle into warm, sterilized jars and cover. Process if liked, seal and label.

## DRIED APRICOT AND ALMOND PRESERVE

### INGREDIENTS

*1½ lb (about 5 cups) ready-to-eat dried apricots, halved*

*1 qt water*

*finely grated zest and juice of ½ lemon*

*finely grated zest of 2 small oranges*

*3 cups sugar*

*½ cup blanched almonds, slivered*

**Makes about 5 pounds**

This is an excellent preserve with a pronounced apricot flavor that can be made at any time of year.

Put the apricots and water into a large pan and simmer over gentle heat until the fruit is very tender – about 1 hour.

Stir in the lemon zest and juice and orange zest. Add the sugar and stir over very gentle heat, or off the heat, until the sugar has dissolved. Stir in the almonds. Raise the heat and boil hard for about 30 minutes or until setting point is reached.

Let the mixture cool to lukewarm, then stir and ladle into warm, sterilized jars. Cover, process if liked, seal and label.

# APPLE OR QUINCE JELLY WITH HERBS

## INGREDIENTS

*6 lb tart apples or ripe quinces, cut up (peel and core included)*

*about 5 pt water*

*sugar*

*handful of fresh thyme, sage or oregano*

**Makes about 5 pounds**

With jelly-making, the general rule is to use 3 cups of sugar for every 3¾ cups of juice. You can, of course, use such proportions for this recipe. However, I find the general rule a little too sweet, so I prefer to use the proportions given here.

Place the fruit in a large pan and barely cover with the water. Simmer until the fruit is soft and pulpy – about 45 minutes.

Wet and wring out a jelly bag if you have one and suspend it over a large bowl. Or make an improvised jelly bag: wet and wring out a large piece of cheesecloth folded into three layers, then tie each corner to the leg of an upturned stool; place a large bowl beneath.

Tip the fruit into the bag and allow the juice to drip for about 10 hours, or overnight if you like. On no account must the bag be squeezed, otherwise pulp will be forced through the cloth and cloud the jelly.

Measure the juice and measure 3 cups of sugar for every 1 quart of juice. Return to the clean pan and stir together over low heat until the sugar has dissolved. Reserve a few sprigs of herbs; tie the rest in a cheesecloth bag and add it to the pan. Raise the heat and boil until setting point is reached, testing after about 10 minutes.

Remove the bag of herbs and discard it. Ladle the jelly into warm, sterilized jars. Add the reserved herbs, boiled briefly, to each jar, stirring to distribute them just as the jelly starts to set. Cover and seal (there is no need to process jellies in a boiling water bath).

*Chunky Marmalade with Whisky (page 43)*

# EYE-OPENERS, PICK-UPS AND PUNCHES

For some the ideal eye-opener is a glass of freshly squeezed orange juice; for others it is a cup of hot, strong coffee. The drinks in this section, however, principally reflect the festive nature of the late breakfast. It is, after all, a break with the humdrum, an occasion to be celebrated.

Freshly squeezed fruit juice provides natural sugar and energy that the body can put to immediate use. When taken on an empty stomach, it also eliminates toxins from the system; such qualities do not exist in pasteurized juices, which are denatured through heating.

Delightful drinks can be made by combining several different types of juice, such as orange and grapefruit. With the aid of an electric juicer, the juice of non-citrus fruit can be easily extracted, so that combinations of, say, apple and grape, or pineapple and orange, melon and strawberry or the classic orange, carrot and apple can be added effortlessly to your repertoire.

If you are nursing a severe hangover, I daresay the best remedial pick-up is water, lots of it, and some Vitamin B. A doctor would certainly not recommend the hair of the dog. However, there exist many so-called remedies, devised by bartenders, based on alcohol. Some of these eye-openers and pick-ups are included in this chapter. The general idea is that if you do not lose your hangover, you will certainly forget it.

## MORNING GLORY FIZZ

### INGREDIENTS

| 1 oz Pernod |
| 2 oz Scotch whisky |
| 2 tbsp egg white, lightly beaten with a fork |
| 2 tsp sugar syrup or superfine sugar |
| juice of ½ lime |
| juice of ½ lemon |
| about 1 cup chilled club soda |

**Fills 4 cocktail glasses**

Dr. Johnson said this famous picker-upper 'will give a good appetite and quiet the nerves.' I find it delicious.

If you like, frost the rims of the glasses by rubbing with a cut lemon or lime, then dipping the rims in sugar. Fill a cocktail shaker one-third full with crushed ice. Add all the ingredients except for the club soda. Shake vigorously for about 2 minutes, then strain into chilled glasses. Stir in the club soda and serve immediately.

## PRAIRIE OYSTER

### INGREDIENTS

| 1 oz Cognac |
| 1 tbsp raspberry vinegar or white wine vinegar |
| about 2 tsp Worcestershire sauce |
| 1 tsp tomato paste or catsup |
| 1 tsp Angostura bitters |

### FOR THE GARNISH

| 1 egg yolk |
| pinch of cayenne |

**Serves 1**

One of the most highly esteemed 'morning after' pick-ups, this contains a raw egg yolk.

Fill a cocktail shaker one-third full with ice cubes. Add all the ingredients, except for the garnish. Shake for about 1 minute. Strain into a glass, and add the whole egg yolk and cayenne. Drink this cocktail in a single gulp, swallowing the egg yolk whole.

## SUISSESSE

### INGREDIENTS

| 2 oz Pernod |
| 1 tsp sugar syrup or superfine sugar |
| 2 tbsp egg white, lightly beaten with a fork |
| juice of 1 lime or ½ lemon |
| ½–1 cup chilled club soda |

### FOR THE GARNISH (OPTIONAL)

| slices of lime or lemon |

**Serves 2 to 4**

This is a great picker-upper or eye-opener for Pernod fans. The lime juice gives it a particularly clean, fresh taste.

Fill a cocktail shaker about one-third full with crushed ice. Add all of the ingredients except for the club soda. Shake vigorously for about 1 minute. Pour the mixture, including the ice, into glasses. Top up with the club soda and serve, garnished with lime or lemon slices if liked.

## BLOODY MARY

### INGREDIENTS

*3 oz vodka*

*1 cup tomato juice*

*juice of ½ lemon*

*salt and freshly ground pepper*

*few drops of Worcestershire sauce*

*dash of hot pepper sauce*

**Serves 2 to 3**

Renowned for its invigorating qualities, a Bloody Mary comes in many guises. This version is my own special favorite, and a good basis from which to establish your own 'specialty.'

Put 10 ice cubes into a cocktail shaker, filling it to one-third full. Add all the ingredients and shake for 30 seconds, then strain into glasses.

## CHAMPAGNE

Almost any Champagne is an instant pick-me-up. First-class Champagne is much more than that; it is a miracle of nature, so I don't like to adulterate it with this and that. However, there are two very popular ways of disguising less than excellent Champagne or sparkling wine, and they are Buck's Fizz, or Mimosa, and Kir Royale. The proportions I give below are a guide, and can naturally be varied to suit personal taste.

*Buck's Fizz or Mimosa*
Allow 1 part orange juice to 4 parts Champagne.

*Kir Royale*
Allow 1 tsp crème de cassis to every ½ cup of Champagne. Put the crème de cassis into the

Champagne glass (or punch bowl) first, then pour the Champagne on top. In this way, you will avoid the need for unnecessary stirring.

## CHAMPAGNE PUNCH

### INGREDIENTS

*3 small ripe pineapples, peeled, cored and roughly chopped*

*2 cups superfine sugar*

*2 cups lemon juice*

*2 cups orange juice*

*2½ cups Cognac*

*2½ cups white rum*

*about ½ cup maraschino liqueur*

*½ cup Curaçao*

*6 bottles chilled Champagne*

**Serves about 24**

The night before, purée the pineapple flesh in a food processor and transfer to a large bowl. Sprinkle over the sugar and leave for an hour or so, then stir in the lemon and orange juices, Cognac, rum, maraschino liqueur and Curaçao. Cover and leave to stand overnight.

Just before the punch is to be served, transfer the pineapple mixture to a punch bowl. Add a block of ice and chilled Champagne.

## NEW ORLEANS PUNCH

### INGREDIENTS

*1 oz rum*

*2 oz bourbon*

*2 oz lemon juice*

*2 oz raspberry syrup*

*1 cup chilled black tea, preferably Earl Grey*

FOR THE GARNISH

*slices of orange*

**Serves 2**

This is an astonishingly good punch, particularly in hot weather. In the absence of raspberry syrup – which can be bought from better supermarkets and liquor stores – purée a can of raspberries in syrup. The punch can be adapted to large quantities if a punch bowl and block of ice replace the cocktail shaker and crushed ice.

Fill a cocktail shaker one-third full with about 6 tablespoons crushed ice. Add all the ingredients, except for the tea. Shake vigorously, then pour the mixture, complete with the ice, into tall glasses. Top up with the tea, and stir with a bar spoon to make the glasses frosty. Garnish with slices of orange and serve.

## PROHIBITION FRUIT PUNCH

### INGREDIENTS

1¾ cups chilled apricot syrup, or 16 oz can apricots in syrup, puréed and chilled

1 cup lime juice, chilled

juice of 1 lemon

2½ cups orange juice, chilled

pinch of salt

1 qt lime-flavored carbonated mineral water or plain club soda

FOR THE GARNISH

slices of orange, lemon and lime

sprigs of mint or borage

**Fills 10 tumblers**

Put all of the ingredients, except for the mineral water or club soda, into a large punch bowl, along with a large block of ice. Moments before serving, stir in the mineral water or club soda, and garnish.

## GRAPEFRUIT AND MINT RICKEY

### INGREDIENTS

½ cup unsweetened grapefruit juice, preferably freshly squeezed

½ tsp mint syrup

juice of ½ lime

about ½ cup lime-flavored carbonated mineral water

**Serves 1**

This is one of my favorite non-alcoholic drinks. It has a fairly sharp, elegant taste, and a ravishingly pretty color.

Fill a tumbler one-third full with ice cubes. Add all the ingredients and stir with a long spoon. If you like, garnish with slices of lime or lemon, but this is by no means essential. When fresh mint is in season, it makes a particularly appropriate addition to the glass.

## TEA, COFFEE AND CHOCOLATE

Most of us know how to make a decent cup of tea and coffee. But perhaps we are not always as adventurous as we might be about trying various blends. For this reason, it makes sense to develop a good relationship with a reputable tea and coffee merchant who will make suggestions, advise and, above all, provide inspiration.

Obvious choices for a strong breakfast tea include Assam, or a blend of Assam or Northern Indian and Ceylon. China Keemun, which was the original 'English Breakfast Tea,' is less brisk and less malty, tending more toward a fragrant nutty flavor. Darjeeling, which is often referred to as the champagne of teas, combines richness of flavor with a subtle bouquet reminiscent of Muscatel.

Fragrant teas are mostly associated with afternoon ceremony. However, I find that blends of Jasmine and Souchong (the latter is often sold as an Orange Pekoe) go well with sweet-tasting breakfast meats such as ham, sausages and bacon.

Another advantage of these teas – and also of certain flower teas such as lime blossom and hibiscus – is that they do not fight with citrus fruit. This can often be a major consideration at breakfast. Remember that larger-leafed tea needs to stand for longer than small-leafed varieties.

The labeling of coffee blends can be very confusing. Names such as Mocha or Continental are used imprecisely and have little meaning. Mocha, which is loosely connected with Italy and espresso coffee, is in fact a port in Yemen, associated with good-quality coffee from Ethiopia. And Continental is merely an all-embracing term that has come to mean a dark heavy roast with a bit of bite to it; it does not describe a type of bean or blend.

Fortunately, there are only two main groups of bean: Arabica and Robusta. Of the two, Robusta is cheaper and less delicate, although in certain blends it can contribute valuable body. Arabica has two main grades, namely washed and unwashed, terms that describe the particular hulling and drying process, which may be wet or dry. Washed (or wet method) Arabica beans are superior because only the ripest coffee cherries are put through the huller; also, generally speaking, the wet method permits tight quality control.

It is vital to know which of these types and grades you are starting with before facing the other issues of regional characteristics and type of roast. Of course your choice is all a matter of personal taste. I happen to like a very strong, but unbitter, espresso coffee with breakfast. What I look for in the first place is 100% washed Arabica beans; next comes the region and flavor type, which in my case might be Brazil; finally comes the roast which, for espresso, is traditionally a very high one.

Robusta is sometimes included in an espresso blend, but I find it makes the coffee taste flat. So much for espresso.

But what if your preference is for a less strong but, nevertheless, rich breakfast coffee that is taken black? Then you may opt for the character of a Colombian style (Arabica) bean with a medium-full roast.

If, on the other hand, your idea of breakfast perfection is a coffee that lends itself well to the addition of milk, true café au lait style, different characteristics should be sought, namely well-defined flavor and a color that looks a rich, full brown – rather than a grey or muddy tone – once the milk is added. Such characteristics may be found in a number of styles, but the one I would suggest is a blend that my coffee merchant Mr. Higgins (of H. R. Higgins, 79 Duke Street, London, W.1) makes for me: equal parts of Costa Rican, Colombian and Tanzanian beans with a medium roast.

Whatever the choice, you will need the right grind for your coffee: fine for filter, medium for *cafetière*, jug and percolator. All coffee will have a better flavor when made from beans that are freshly ground. If the beans have been stored in the freezer or in the refrigerator, they will profit from being warmed very gently in the oven before being ground. Freshly drawn, cold water is essential to good coffee. If your water supply is affected by chlorine, then consider using a water filter or using bottled spring water instead.

Making large quantities of coffee and keeping it hot without spoiling when entertaining does not have to be a problem if you employ vacuum jugs.

Despite the present-day popularity of tea and coffee, chocolate was the favorite in the eighteenth century. A typical brew is as follows: melt 3 ounces broken dark chocolate in a splash of hot water, then add 3¾ cups hot milk. Bring to a boil, stirring once or twice, and simmer for 15–30 minutes. Remove from the heat, whisk well and serve. Popular additions include rum, brandy, whipped cream, nutmeg, cinnamon, grated orange zest and prepared coffee.

# A

# *Victorian*

## CORNISH
## HOUSE PARTY

The splendors of the Victorian breakfast were vividly recalled in *Memories of Three Reigns* by Lady Raglan, wife of Field Marshal Lord Raglan, who commanded the British forces in the Crimea. Writing of a Cornish house-party breakfast of 1870 during the shooting season, she described a table breathtaking in its scope and notable in its selection of meats.

'There would be a choice of fish, fried eggs and crisp bacon, a variety of egg dishes, omelets and sizzling sausages and bacon. During the shooting season hot game and grilled pheasants were always served, but of course without any vegetables. On a side table was always to be found a choice of cold meats: delicious home-smoked hams, pressed meats, one of the large raised pies for which Mrs. Vaughan (the cook) was justly famous, consisting of cold game and galantine with aspic jelly. The guests drank either tea or coffee, and there were invariable accompaniments of home-made rolls (piping hot) and stillroom preserves of apple and quince jelly; and always piled bowls of rich Cornish cream. The meal usually finished with a fruit course of grapes and hothouse peaches and nectarines.'

The task of preparing such a large repast may appear daunting for the modern cook who may lack the necessary help in the kitchen. In any case, a house-party menu today usually has to be tailored to suit leaner resources. This one can easily be reduced to a smaller scale by selecting just a few of the items.

A ham is generally a sensible choice for large weekend parties. Not only can it be prepared in advance – perhaps served hot for dinner the night before; it also allows a lot of people to help themselves to food whenever they wish. The same can be said of a large raised pie, which may be filled with game when there is a glut of it.

*Selection of Eye-Openers, Pick-Ups
and Punches*

*Home-made Pork and Sage Sausages
Bacon
Selection of Egg Dishes*

*Ham with Cider, Orange, Cloves and
Honey
or
Raised Game Pie
or
Roasted Pheasant or Broiled Quail
or
Deviled Kidneys with Maître
d'Hôtel Butter*

*Peach and Nectarine Salad or Fresh
Grapes*

*Selection of Preserves, Breads, Rolls
and Muffins
Thick Cream   Honey*

*Coffee or Tea*

If advance preparation does not fit in with your schedule, then hot, broiled or roasted game can provide more or less instant fare. You could also consider serving some unusual Spicy Scrambled Eggs (page 16). These have hot seasonings of turmeric and coriander, which were very fashionable in the nineteenth century.

Out of the game season, a Cornish breakfast table would have made more play of local fish, such as the plentiful pilchard and mackerel. These would have been broiled and served plain. Cod or whiting would have been as likely to turn up in the form of fish cakes. You can make them by following the recipe for Salmon Fish Cakes with a Tomato and Caper Sauce (page 40), and substituting white fish. They can be partly prepared in advance and finished a few moments before the guests require them.

It is unlikely that haddock would have found its way on to a Cornish table, unless brought by a guest from the North of England or Scotland. However, a contemporary cook might consider preparing a Traditional Kedgeree of Smoked Finnan Haddie (page 117), as it is an excellent dish for a large number of people. Another departure from Lady Raglan's menu would be the Deviled Kidneys. This recipe is borrowed from the breakfast fare at Plumstead Episcopi, the bishop's village described by Anthony Trollope in *The Warden*, in 1855. Kidneys were a firm favorite for breakfast in the nineteenth century.

The sizzling sausages to which Lady Raglan refers were surely home-made. My recipe is for a classic combination of pork and sage. The casings must be ordered in advance from your butcher; be sure to order the right sort for the size of sausage you want. A casing of pig's intestine is the right shape for the average sized sausage, while lamb's intestines – which are very narrow – suit smaller sausages. Relatively wide ox intestines make fatter sausages.

However, casings are not essential. Certainly many nineteenth-century Cornish sausages would have been skinless, like the Oxford ones that generally included some minced veal along with the pork. These are much faster to make since the meat does not have to be passed through a mincing machine and into the casing. All you need do is grind the meat in a food processor – which takes seconds – and shape the meat by hand. In my view, the resultant sausage meat also finishes with a better color for having been chopped cleanly with the processor's sharp blades rather than squeezed through the mincer.

Perhaps certain guests would have opted for the finale alone. I have assembled peaches and nectarines, along with a few almonds, into a salad with a syrup tinged blush-pink by the skins of the fruit. The fruit course was taken very seriously by the Victorians, who took great pride in growing exotic fruits in their hothouses, more or less exclusively for the pleasures of breakfast. If you are being economical with time, the salad could be made in extra quantity and served at another meal. It would have been served with the wonderful Cornish cream, thick and crusty, which was a feature of breakfasts in the West Country. This would have been spread liberally over the breads and muffins and so on, in place of butter, with preserves spooned over the top.

# HOME-MADE PORK AND SAGE SAUSAGES

## INGREDIENTS

6 ft sausage casing

juice of ½ lemon

2 lb pork shoulder butt, boned, trimmed and cut into pieces

½ lb boned loin of pork, cut into pieces

1 ½ tbsp finely chopped fresh sage, or mixed sage and parsley

1 tsp salt

freshly ground pepper

¼ tsp ground mace

¼ tsp freshly grated nutmeg

**Makes ten 5-inch sausages weighing about 2 pounds**

The fun of sausages is that you can flavor and shape them as you wish. Apart from the pork and sage combination I have chosen, you could also try lamb and mint, or beef and thyme, or a mixture of pork, veal, thyme and parsley. And instead of making individual sausages linked to each other by a twist in the casing, try filling a long length of casing that can be coiled around itself, rather like a Catherine wheel, to make a large spiral sausage about the size of a frying pan. This style of sausage makes an eye-catching presentation; slice across it to yield individual helpings.

Start by soaking the casing for 30 minutes in water to cover, with the lemon juice; drain. Rinse the casing inside and out by inserting a funnel or nozzle into one end and pouring in cold water. If the casing displays holes, cut out and discard the torn section. Drain the casing but do not pat it dry; set aside.

Pass the meat through the medium disc of a meat grinder. Transfer the meat to a bowl, add the herbs and seasonings and mix well. Fry a little of the raw mixture, taste it and adjust the seasoning if necessary.

Ease one end of the casing on to the nozzle of the sausage-making attachment of a mincer, sausage-making machine or electric grinder. Gradually push, and gather up the casing on to the nozzle, until you are left with 5 inches of casing hanging free. Knot the end. Pass the meat through the mincer, easing the casing as it falls away from the nozzle. When the casing is filled to within a finger's length of its end, detach and knot it. With your hands, roll the sausage to and fro on the work surface to distribute the contents evenly.

To form individual sausages, first decide on the length of sausage you want, then when the casing is full to the appropriate length, twist it through a complete turn. Twist alternate links after that in opposite directions; this will prevent the sausages from unwinding. Prick the skin of each sausage in several places. Cut linked sausages into separate ones.

To fry the sausages, cover the bottom of a frying pan with a little water and bring it to the boil. Add the sausages and fry them, turning them frequently, for about 15 minutes. During this time, the water will evaporate, and the sausages will then cook in their own exuded fat. You may prefer, however, to omit the water and, instead, fry the sausages in a little oil. To broil the sausages, turn them frequently under a medium heat for about 15 minutes or until they are cooked through and browned all over.

# HAM WITH CIDER,
## ORANGE, CLOVES AND HONEY

This method of preparing ham can easily be adapted for smaller portions. For half a ham, slightly reduce the flavoring ingredients used for poaching and halve the ingredients for finishing the ham.

Whatever its size, soak the ham for at least 8 hours, changing the water several times. Then place it in a very large ham kettle or pot, add the wine and pour over enough fresh cold water just to cover the meat. Add the flavorings for poaching. Over a medium heat, bring the liquid to simmering point. Put on the lid set slightly askew, and adjust the heat to maintain an extremely gentle simmer so that the surface of the liquid barely trembles. Poach the ham allowing 15 minutes per pound. Top up the liquid with fresh cold water from time to time to ensure that the ham is always just covered.

Remove the ham from the liquid and, when it is cool enough to handle, remove the strings and peel away any rind. Lightly score the fat lengthwise at regular 1¾-inch intervals; then score diagonally across, to make diamond shapes. Transfer to a roasting pan. Combine the cider, orange zest and juice and 4 tablespoons of the honey. Brush some of this mixture over the ham, and pour the remainder around it. Stud the ham fat at the points of the diamonds with cloves. Cover the top of the leg bone with foil to prevent it from burning.

Preheat the oven to 375°. Bake the ham for 15 minutes, then baste it with the cider mixture in the pan. Loosely cover with foil, lower the heat to 350° and bake for a further 45 minutes. Lift the foil and baste at 15 minute intervals during this time. About 5 minutes before the end of cooking, you may, if you wish, intensify the glaze: to do this, remove the foil, raise the oven temperature to 400° and brush the ham with the remaining honey. Return to the oven to bake for 5 to 10 minutes. During this time, watch the ham very carefully as the honey may burn.

Transfer the ham to a serving platter and let it rest for about 30 minutes, loosely covered with foil, before carving it. Remove the foil from the ham bone and replace it with a paper frill. Serve warm or cold. The basting juices may be strained, degreased and served as an accompaniment, along with sage-flavored apple jelly.

## INGREDIENTS

1 ham, lightly smoked, weighing about 20 lb and tied into a neat shape

Apple Jelly with Sage (page 19), to serve

### FOR POACHING THE HAM

1½ cups medium-dry white wine

2 tsp juniper berries, lightly bruised

2 tsp black peppercorns, lightly bruised

2 tsp coriander seeds

3 large sprigs fresh thyme

3 bay leaves

### FOR FINISHING THE HAM

1¼ cups medium-dry hard cider

grated zest and juice of 2 large oranges or 3 smaller ones

4–6 tbsp liquid honey

50–60 cloves

**Serves about 24**

# RAISED GAME PIE

## INGREDIENTS

### FOR THE JELLIED STOCK

3 cups Gelatinous Veal Stock
(page 32)

⅔ cup malmsey Madeira or port
wine

### FOR THE PASTRY

7¼ cups all-purpose flour

½ tsp salt

14 oz (3½ sticks) unsalted butter,
finely diced

4 large egg yolks

2 pinches of cayenne

about 2 cups cold water

1 egg yolk mixed with 3 tbsp
water, for the glaze

### FOR THE FILLING

breasts and legs of 3 pheasants

5 ¼-in thick slices cooked ham

2¼ lb reserved pheasant livers,
supplemented by chicken livers

3¼ lb lean boneless pork

14 oz fatty boneless pork

2 tbsp crushed juniper berries

1½ cups Cognac

finely grated zest of 3 oranges

1 cup orange juice

2 tsp freshly grated nutmeg

2 large pinches of ground
cinnamon

about 5 tsp dried thyme

salt and freshly ground pepper

¼ cup shelled and peeled pistachio
nuts (optional)

Almost any type of game — except perhaps very small birds — can be used to make a pie of this sort. A mixture of hare and partridge is very good. The quantities can be halved or even quartered. The flavor of the binding jelly is a matter of personal choice, some people preferring the unassertive flavor of veal-stock jelly to the stronger flavor of game-stock jelly, others the opposite.

A day or two before making the pie, prepare the stock. Set aside the measured amount for the game pie; freeze the remainder for future use.

Since there is a large amount of pastry, you may find it easier to make it up in two batches. Sift the flour and salt into a bowl and rub in the butter to make large crumbs. Make a well in the center and drop in the egg yolks and cayenne. Gradually mix in enough of the water to create a firm, smooth dough. Weigh the dough and set aside about 1 pound — approximately one-third — for the lid and trimmings. Form the remaining dough into a ball; wrap this, and the dough for the lid separately, in plastic wrap and chill for at least 1 hour.

Bone and skin the pheasants. If you like, reserve the bones for the stock or for game-flavored jelly (opposite page). Cut the boned breast and thigh meat into ¼- to ½-inch strips; reserve the trimmings and lower-leg meat for the forcemeat. Cut the ham into similar sized strips and set all the strips aside. In batches, work the trimmings, lower-leg meat, game livers and chicken livers, pork and crushed juniper berries in a food processor or meat grinder to make a fairly fine forcemeat. Transfer the forcemeat to a bowl. Add the Cognac, orange zest and juice, nutmeg, cinnamon, thyme, salt and pepper to taste, and pistachios if you are using them. Mix well. Cover and leave to marinate for 1 to 2 hours.

When you are ready to line and fill the mold, brush a very thin layer of softened butter or oil around the inside of the mold. Roll out the larger portion of dough to an even thickness, and use it to line the mold, pressing the dough gently into the mold's curves and contours, and making sure there are no cracks. Trim the top edge of dough flush with the mold, so that the sides of the mold can ultimately be removed without disturbing the pastry. Press the chilled sheets of pork fatback to the sides of the dough. Chill the mold for 30 minutes.

Fill the mold with alternate ½-inch thick layers of force-meat, game strips, forcemeat and ham strips. Finish with a layer of forcemeat, piled into a slight dome above the mold's rim. Tap the mold on a work surface to settle the contents.

Roll out about four-fifths of the smaller portion of dough to make a lid about ½ inch thick. Brush the exposed rim of dough with water and place the lid on top, pressing the edges together. If you like, make a pattern around the edge using a fork. Do make sure that the rim of the mold is free of dough, to ensure trouble-free unmolding. Cut a hole in the center of the lid and insert a funnel or a piece of card. Use the remaining dough to make decorative pastry crescents or leaves and a rosette or plug of some kind to conceal the hole when the pie is presented. I sometimes make the plug in the shape of a bird, using peppercorns for its eyes. Stick the decorations in place with a small amount of the egg yolk glaze. Put the rosette or plug on a baking sheet to bake separately. Transfer everything to the refrigerator and chill for at least 30 minutes.

Preheat the oven to 425°. Bake the pie and rosette for 15 minutes, then cover the lid with foil, reduce the heat to 350° and bake the pie for a further 1¾ hours (1¼ hours if the pie is considerably smaller than the dimensions I have given), removing the rosette after about 20 minutes. Remove the foil and brush the lid with the egg yolk glaze. Return the pie to the oven to bake for a further 10 to 15 minutes or until the top is golden brown. Remove and cool at room temperature. Undo the side clips of the mold, and gently remove the sides. If the pastry beneath is not brown and crisp, glaze it and return to the oven to bake for a further 10 minutes or so. Allow to cool to tepid.

Gently melt the stock and stir in the Madeira. The mixture should be just tepid. Pour it through the hole in the top of the pie, then remove the funnel. When the pie has cooled completely, chill it to set the stock to a jelly.

Present the pie with the rosette or other plug placed over the hole. Keep in a cool airy place.

## A NOTE ON GAME STOCK AND THE FLAVOR OF THE JELLY

To make a gelatinous game stock, combine the veal stock with the broken-up game carcasses and bones, and simmer these ingredients over very gentle heat, with the lid of the pan askew, for 1 to 2 hours. Strain, cool and degrease the stock, at which point it is ready for use. For the game pie, you would require only about 3 cups of gelatinous game stock, but bear in mind that you would have to use at least 5 cups of veal stock to cover the game carcasses. Personally, I would not want to flavor more veal stock with game than was absolutely necessary, since veal stock is such a marvelously useful all-purpose stock, but you could refrigerate the extra game stock until it sets to a jelly, turn it out of its bowl, dice it and serve it with the pie.

### FOR THE LINING

*enough thinly sliced pork fatback to line the mold (ask the butcher to slice it on his machine), chilled*

**Fits an eye-shaped game pie or pâté mold 5 inches tall and about 14 inches long; serves 20 to 30**

*Raised Game Pie*

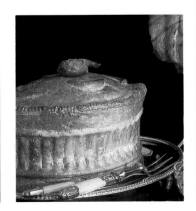

# ROASTED PHEASANT

## INGREDIENTS

*allow ½ pheasant, trussed and barded with pork fatback, per person*

*small amount of olive oil*

*salt and freshly ground pepper*

### FOR THE GARNISH

*watercress*

Writing on pheasant, Brillat-Savarin, the eighteenth-century gastronome, declared: 'Its flesh is tender, sublime and highly flavoured.' I echo his sentiments entirely, but if you have the choice the hen has a finer flavor than the cock. If you are given a brace that includes one of each sex, roast the hen and casserole the cock or use it in a pie.

Pheasant meat is very lean and needs barding with pork fatback. Don't be tempted to use bacon; its strong flavor will compete with that of the pheasant.

Preheat the oven to 450°. Brush the exposed surface of the birds with a little olive oil. Season with salt and freshly ground pepper. Roast for 20 minutes. Remove the barding, then return the pheasants to the oven for a further 5 minutes to brown the breasts.

To carve a pheasant, cut off the legs, then divide each leg in two at the joint. Cut off the wings. Carve each side of the breast into slices. Serve each person with a portion of leg, a wing and slices of meat from the breast. Garnish with watercress. You can also serve the pheasant livers, lightly cooked then mashed, on toast.

# GELATINOUS VEAL STOCK

## INGREDIENTS

*1 calf's foot, halved or quartered depending on size, then blanched in simmering water for 5 minutes and drained*

*3 lb veal shank*

*2 carrots*

*1 medium onion, halved and each half stuck with 2 cloves*

*4 large garlic cloves, crushed*

*1 large bouquet garni including fresh thyme, parsley, bay and citrus peel*

*salt*

**Makes 3 quarts (about 10½ cups)**

Veal stock is the most versatile of all stocks. It not only has a mild unassertive flavor that complements a wide range of meat and poultry dishes, it also sets to a firm jelly. It is well worth making a large quantity and freezing the excess in half-pint containers.

Put the blanched calf's foot and veal shank in a large pan. Add enough water just to cover the ingredients and bring to the boil very slowly, with the lid of the pan set askew. Remove the scum that rises to the surface. Add a wine glass of water and bring back to the boil, skimming off the scum again; repeat until no more scum rises. Wipe the sides of the pan clean.

Add the vegetables, garlic, bouquet garni and a pinch of salt. Return to the boil again, very slowly, then skim once more. Set the lid askew and adjust the heat so that the liquid barely simmers. Leave to cook for about 5 hours.

Strain the stock through a cheesecloth-lined colander set over a large bowl; discard the solids. Taste the stock and add salt. Cool the stock to room temperature, then refrigerate until set. Degrease the jellied stock by scraping the fat from the surface, then wipe away the last traces of fat with a cloth dipped in hot water and squeezed dry. The stock is now ready to use. Measure what you need for immediate use and freeze the rest.

# BROILED QUAIL

To make the birds a suitable shape for even and rapid cooking, spatchcock them: cut along one side of the backbone of each quail with poultry shears or strong scissors, then cut down the other side and discard the bone. Open each bird out and flatten it by pressing on the breastbone with the palm of your hand. Season the birds and brush them with oil. Arrange them, skin side up, on a rack set over a broiler pan.

Preheat the broiler to hot. Cook the birds for 12 minutes, lowering the heat to medium or moving the birds further away from the source of heat after 3 or 4 minutes. Turn and cook the birds for a further 8 minutes or so, until cooked through.

Serve the birds straight away, garnished if you like with watercress or parsley. A red currant jelly or sauce, or spiced oranges, makes a good accompaniment. You can also serve the birds on toast spread with butter and cooked, mashed livers of game or chicken.

## A SIMPLE STUFFING

The birds can be attractively plumped up with stuffing beneath their breasts (see picture below) before you broil them, but you can only stuff the birds in this way if the breast skin is undamaged by gun shot.

One of my favorite stuffings is quickly made in a food processor: simply put 3 slices of broken-up white bread and ¼ pound game or chicken livers, plus a good pinch of dried thyme, into the bowl of a food processor and blend for a few seconds. Combine this mixture with 4 tablespoons of butter, mashed with a fork. Season with salt and pepper. This makes enough for 4 to 6 birds.

## INGREDIENTS

allow 1 quail, cleaned and
  untrussed, per person

salt and freshly ground pepper

small amount of olive oil

### FOR THE GARNISH

watercress or parsley

*Broiled Quail*

# DEVILED KIDNEYS
## WITH MAITRE D'HOTEL BUTTER

### INGREDIENTS

8 lambs' kidneys, trimmed of
  excess fat and connective tissue

salt and freshly ground pepper

about 5 tbsp butter, melted

### FOR THE DEVIL MIXTURE

2 tsp prepared English (hot)
  mustard

4 tbsp Worcestershire sauce

several pinches of cayenne

1/3 cup fine dried bread crumbs

### FOR THE MAITRE D'HOTEL BUTTER (OPTIONAL)

1 stick unsalted butter, softened

1 tbsp finely chopped fresh parsley

salt and freshly ground pepper

1 tsp lemon juice

### FOR THE GARNISH

broiled tomatoes

watercress

**Serves 8**

Victorian empire-builders had grown to appreciate hot spicy flavors after living in India; and they transferred this appreciation to Deviled Kidneys. This deviled brew, however, is more piquant than desperately hot and fiery.

If you intend to serve a maître d'hôtel butter with the kidneys, prepare it first: mash the softened butter thoroughly with a fork until smooth, then work in the parsley, seasoning and lemon juice. Form into neat pats and chill in the refrigerator or freezer until very firm.

Preheat the broiler to medium.

Cut the kidneys almost horizontally through without separating the halves, so that each opens out into a butterfly shape. Trim away excess core. Season and paint with melted butter. Then cook under the broiler for about 1 minute on each side. Thread the kidneys on to skewers.

Mix together the mustard, Worcestershire sauce and cayenne in a shallow dish or soup plate. Spread out the bread crumbs on a separate plate. Dip the kidneys first in the mustard mixture, then coat with bread crumbs. Strain and reserve any remaining mustard mixture to serve separately. Broil for 3 to 4 minutes on each side Serve the kidneys on toast: maître d'hôtel butter lends a contrasting calm suavity to the hot kidneys; tomatoes and watercress make a colorful garnish.

*Deviled Kidneys with Maître d'Hôtel Butter*

# PEACH AND NECTARINE SALAD

Choose fruit with the pinkest of skins, so that when the skins are boiled with the syrup they give it a natural pink blush.

Loosen the skins of the fruit by scoring them lightly around the middle and plunging the fruit briefly into boiling water, then into cold. Remove the skins and set them aside for use in the syrup. Cut the fruits in half and pick out the pits. Crush the pits to free the kernels, then wrap the kernels in cheesecloth and set aside. Cut the fruit into quarters, or eighths if they are extra large and extra firm.

Put the sugar and water into a large heavy-based saucepan. Stir over a gentle heat until the sugar has dissolved, then raise the heat and bring the syrup to the boil without stirring. Let the syrup boil for several minutes, then lower the heat to maintain a gentle simmer. Add the kernels and the fruit, lowering the fruit into the syrup using a large spoon. Simmer the fruit until it is tender but still holding its shape; this will take from a few minutes up to 20, depending on the ripeness of the fruit. Remove pieces of fruit as they are done, using a slotted spoon to transfer them to a plate to cool.

Raise the heat, add the reserved fruit skins to the syrup and boil it hard for at least 5 minutes or until the skins have given up their flavor and color to the syrup. Strain the syrup through a strainer set over a bowl – preferably a metal one. Discard the skins, but reserve the bag of kernels. Place the bowl of syrup in a large bowl of iced water to cool it rapidly.

When the syrup is cold, stir in the tiniest pinch of salt and the lemon juice. If you wish, remove the kernels from the cheesecloth and add them to the syrup – they will lend a bitter almond flavor.

Add the fruit and turn it very gently in the syrup, taking care not to break it. The addition of sweet almonds, scattered about the fruit, is an excellent one, though not essential. You can also decorate the salad with a few rose petals. Serve the salad very lightly chilled or at room temperature, with cream and cookies.

## INGREDIENTS

| |
|---|
| 4 firm peaches |
| 4 firm nectarines |
| 1 ½ cups sugar |
| 1 ¾ cups water |
| pinch of salt |
| juice of 1 small lemon |
| 3–4 tbsp slivered almonds (optional) |
| cream and cookies such as almond or shortbread, to serve |

**Serves 8**

# A

## *High land*

### F L I N G

When Daniel Defoe visited Scotland in 1707 he noted 'salmon in such plenty as is scarce credible.' I mention this by way of justification since salmon appears on this menu twice, once in smoked form and once in fresh. As a further softener, perhaps I should add that the Smoked Salmon Packages are not as prohibitively expensive as they may appear since you do not need much salmon to envelop the scrambled eggs (the recipe appears on page 123). However, the slices do need to be long enough to provide a proper wrapping; thus, pre-packaged smoked salmon is an unwise choice, because you cannot see the size of the slices.

The fresh Salmon Fish Cakes with a Tomato and Caper Sauce are humbler but a truly excellent match. The clean flavor of the sauce, accentuated by a little sharpness from the capers, forms a flattering partnership with the fish and its breadcrumb coating. If you do not have time to make the sauce, you can serve the fish cakes by themselves or with a home-made mayonnaise enlivened with dill or fennel and some chopped tomato. A thriftier but good version of the cakes can be made using white fish, such as cod or pike.

Any true Scottish breakfast menu must surely include proper porridge made with oatmeal rather than processed porridge oats. Recipes may call for medium or coarse oatmeal, the latter producing a grainier porridge. Coarse oatmeal generally requires longer cooking or an overnight soaking, or sometimes both, depending on personal choice. Some people like their porridge cooked briefly to the preliminary stage of graininess; others like it taken through an intermediate stage of creaminess; then there are others who insist on an advanced stage of cooking, so that the porridge becomes very smooth.

My recipes tend toward the grainy and creamy. The Thick Grainy Porridge with Coarse Oatmeal comes from

# SALMON FISH CAKES WITH TOMATO AND CAPER SAUCE

*Selection of Eye-Openers, Pick-Ups and Punches*

*Compote of Fresh and Dried Fruit*
*or*
*Highland Porridge with Medium Oatmeal*
*or*
*Thick Grainy Porridge*

*Salmon Fish Cakes*
*Tomato and Caper Sauce*
*or*
*Smoked Salmon Packages*
*or*
*Ham and Haddie or Finnan Haddie*

*An Old-fashioned Orange Cream*

*Scottish Oatcakes*
*or*
*Selection of Breads, Rolls and Muffins*
*Chunky Marmalade with Whisky*

*Coffee or Tea*

Margaret Sweetnam, who helped me test the recipes in this book.

Once the porridge is on the table the accompaniments are again down to personal choice. Whatever you put on it is 'correct' if you happen to like it: salt, sugar or, more unusually, dried fruits, cinnamon and honey which, despite immediate associations with the contemporary muesli habit, go back in history to frumenty, an ancient cousin of porridge made from husked or pearled wheat.

Another 'must' on a Scottish menu is finnan haddie. Its unique flavor is said to be due to a happy accident that occurred many years ago, when a catch of fresh haddock was being salt-cured in a small curing house in north-east Scotland. A fire broke out, filling the house with smoke. When it eventually died down, the fish was examined and sampled. The flesh was deliciously smoky – so good that it soon became considered a delicacy. Genuine finnan haddie is pale yellow in color, and must not be confused with brighter imitations, which have been dyed. I like to poach it in milk in the oven – as in the recipe for Ham and Haddie. This keeps it moist and draws out any sharp saltiness.

Kippers are another great specialty of Scotland. Small ones are best and have the finest flavor; these do not require a preliminary parboiling. To broil them, simply wipe them with a damp cloth, rub them with a little butter, then broil each side for a few minutes or until they are crisped to your liking.

I have included a sweet cream because the Scots have a tradition for them. Samuel Johnson declared when he visited Scotland in 1775: 'In the place of tarts, there are always set different preparations of milk.' He was referring to the possets, syllabubs, custards and creams of the day. I think he would have approved of this Orange Cream. It has a light texture that allows the fresh flavor of the orange to emerge.

None of the main courses in this menu take long to prepare and all may be done before breakfast. But the oatmeal for the Thick Grainy Porridge with Coarse Oatmeal needs soaking overnight and the oatcakes must be started the day before. You can also partially prepare the fish cakes in advance, and the Compote of Fresh and Dried Fruit and Orange Cream improve in flavor if they are made the day before. The Scottish marmalade can only be made when Seville oranges are in season, around January.

# COMPOTE OF FRESH AND DRIED FRUIT

Put the dried fruit and sugar into a large saucepan. Pour the wine over. Bring to a simmer, stirring gently to dissolve the sugar, then partially cover the pan and let the mixture simmer gently for 5 minutes.

Meanwhile, peel the rind and white pith from the oranges, then slice the flesh. Add the orange slices to the pan, together with the honey. The fruit should be just immersed in liquid so add a little water if necessary. Partially cover the pan again and let the mixture simmer for a further 20 minutes.

Remove the pan from the heat and leave to cool, preferably by standing the base of the pan in iced water. When the compote is completely cold, taste it and stir in more honey or sugar if necessary. Turn into a bowl, cover and chill for at least 1 hour, and up to 24 hours.

About 5 to 10 minutes before serving, spoon the compote into a decorative dish. Add the almonds and allow to stand briefly at room temperature before serving.

### INGREDIENTS

1 ½ lb mixed ready-to-eat dried fruit including apricots, pears, figs and prunes

¾ cup sugar

1 bottle Sauternes or other sweet white wine

2 large oranges

1 tbsp clear honey

¼ cup blanched almonds, coarsely chopped

**Serves 6 to 8**

# HIGHLAND PORRIDGE
## WITH MEDIUM OATMEAL

True British oatmeal, in fine, medium and coarse grinds, is available in some specialty stores in the United States. If you cannot obtain it, use coarse Scotch or Irish oats to make the porridge, and adjust the liquid quantities and cooking times accordingly.

*A quick method*
In a heavy saucepan, mix together the oatmeal, water and salt until smooth. Bring to the boil over medium heat, then simmer very gently for about 25 minutes, stirring frequently, and adding a little more water if you like a thinner porridge.

*A longer method*
Put the water and salt in a saucepan and bring to the boil. Sprinkle in the oatmeal gradually, beating with a whisk all the time to prevent lumps forming. When the porridge has thickened to your liking, lower the heat, cover the pan and leave the porridge to simmer very gently, on an asbestos pad set over a low heat, for about 1 hour. During this time, add a little more water if the porridge becomes too thick for your personal taste. The porridge may also be transferred to a double-boiler once it has thickened, so that it simmers in a trouble-free way over indirect heat.

### INGREDIENTS

1 ¼ cups imported medium-ground oatmeal

3¾ cups water

large pinch of salt

**Serves 4 to 6**

# THICK GRAINY PORRIDGE
## WITH COARSE OATMEAL

### INGREDIENTS

1 ⅛ cups imported coarse-ground
   oatmeal (see page 39)

2 ⅛ cups water

small pinch of salt (optional)

**Serves 4 to 6**

Put the oatmeal and water into a heavy saucepan. Cover and leave to soak overnight. Next morning, add the salt and bring to the boil, stirring constantly. Cook quickly for about 10 minutes over medium to high heat to dry out the porridge and reach the desired thick, grainy consistency.

*Some accompaniments for Porridge*
Honey, syrup, sugar or jam; butter and a little salt; cream, milk or yogurt; chopped dates or raisins; a pinch of cinnamon.

# SALMON FISH CAKES

### INGREDIENTS

1 lb fresh salmon on the bone

flavorings of lemon peel, parsley
   stems and bay leaf

juice of ½ lemon

salt and freshly ground pepper

½ lb potatoes

3 tbsp finely chopped fresh parsley

pinch of cayenne

¼ tsp anchovy paste (optional)

1 tbsp unsalted butter, softened

about ¼ cup warmed milk

### FOR COOKING

about 3 tbsp all-purpose flour
   seasoned with salt and pepper

1 extra large egg, beaten

about 4 tbsp fine, dried white
   bread crumbs

½ lb (2 sticks) unsalted butter,
   clarified to yield about ⅝ cup

2 tbsp light olive or sunflower oil

### FOR SERVING

Tomato and Caper Sauce

wedges of lemon

sprigs of parsley

**Serves 4**

Prepare the Tomato and Caper Sauce (opposite page) but do not add the capers or butter.

To make the fish cakes, preheat the oven to 350°. Enclose the salmon, flavorings, lemon juice and seasoning in a lightly buttered foil package. Cook in the oven for about 20 minutes or until the salmon is just done. Discard the foil wrapping and flavorings, then flake the salmon, discarding the bones and skin. You should be left with about 12 ounces of flaked fish.

Peel the potatoes and cook them in boiling salted water until tender. Drain, then purée through a food mill or potato ricer.

In a large bowl, combine the fish, potatoes, parsley, cayenne, anchovy paste and softened butter. Mix well. Season to taste, then gradually add just enough warmed milk to loosen the mixture slightly.

Flour your hands, then divide and shape the fish mixture into eight cakes, each about 2 inches across and ¾ inches thick. Pat the surfaces of each cake smooth with a palette knife or narrow spatula. If you like, you can keep the fish cakes, covered with plastic wrap, in the refrigerator for several hours or overnight. When you wish to complete the fish cakes, have ready some clarified butter and oil for frying. Roll the fish cakes in seasoned flour and dust off the excess, brush each cake with beaten egg, then coat it with bread crumbs.

Bring the Tomato and Caper Sauce to the boil and add the capers. Keep it warm.

Heat the clarified butter and oil in a heavy frying pan and fry the fish cakes for about 2 minutes on each side or until golden brown. Remove and drain briefly on paper towels. Complete the sauce by whisking in the butter off the heat. Serve the fish cakes hot, garnished with lemon wedges, a few extra capers and sprigs of parsley. You can, if you like, deep-fry the parsley. Pour the sauce around the fish cakes or serve it separately.

# TOMATO AND CAPER SAUCE

Pass the tomatoes through the finest blade of a food mill, set directly over a large saucepan. Add the sugar, marjoram and pepper to taste. Boil the sauce briskly to reduce it to about 1¼ cups, stirring from time to time to prevent sticking. While the sauce is reducing, finely chop half of the capers; leave the remainder whole. Set the capers aside.

Pass the reduced tomato purée through a nylon sieve, rinse out the pan and return the purée to the pan. Stir in the cream. Bring the sauce to the boil and add the chopped and whole capers. Continue to simmer for a few minutes to allow the capers to flavor the sauce. Taste and adjust the seasoning. Just before serving, remove the sauce from the heat and whisk in the cold diced butter.

### INGREDIENTS

| |
|---|
| 4 cups drained canned tomatoes, or 2 lb flavorsome fresh tomatoes |
| ½ tsp sugar |
| 1 tbsp dried marjoram |
| freshly ground pepper |
| 2 tbsp capers, drained and patted dry |
| 3 tbsp heavy cream |
| salt |
| 1 tbsp cold, unsalted butter, diced |

**Makes about 1 ½ cups**

# HAM AND HADDIE

This is a pleasant assembly of slices of ham rolled around cooked, flaked finnan haddie, then topped with white sauce and finished in the oven. For plain finnan haddie, simply follow the instructions for baking the fish in milk. You can serve it just as it is, whole, or you can fillet it before serving. Add a poached egg or bacon, according to your whim.

Start by making the béchamel sauce: melt the butter in a saucepan, stir in the flour and cook for a few minutes, then raise the heat and pour in the milk, whisking constantly to blend the mixture perfectly smooth as it comes to the boil. Immediately reduce the heat to the lowest setting, and leave the sauce to simmer very gently for about 30 minutes, stirring occasionally.

While the sauce simmers, cook the fish. Preheat the oven to 400°. Butter a shallow ovenproof dish. Open up the haddock so that it is flat. Lay the fish skin side up in the dish. Add the flavorings and enough milk barely to immerse the fish. Press buttered foil on top. Cook in the oven for 15 minutes. Turn the fish over, replace the foil and cook for a further 5 minutes.

Drain and cool the fish, then take the flesh off the bone and flake it. If the fish exudes liquid, discard it or it will water down the béchamel in the final assembly. Roll up the fish in the slices of ham and arrange snugly in a shallow ovenproof dish.

Season the béchamel with very little salt (the fish is salty), and pepper and nutmeg to taste. Stir in the chopped parsley and immediately pour the sauce over the Ham and Haddie. Either serve the dish immediately or set it beneath a hot broiler for about 1½ minutes, to color the surface.

### INGREDIENTS

| |
|---|
| 1 finnan haddie or other smoked, firm-fleshed fish on the bone, weighing about 1 lb |
| 8 slices smoked ham, weighing about 10 oz in total |

#### FOR COOKING THE FISH

| |
|---|
| 1 tbsp unsalted butter |
| flavorings of bay leaf, lemon peel and parsley stems |
| 1¾ cups milk |

#### FOR THE BÉCHAMEL SAUCE

| |
|---|
| 3 tbsp unsalted butter |
| 3 tbsp all-purpose flour |
| 1¼ pt milk |
| salt and freshly ground pepper |
| 1–2 pinches of freshly grated nutmeg |
| 3–4 tbsp finely chopped fresh parsley, preferably flat-leaved |

**Serves 4**

# AN OLD-FASHIONED ORANGE CREAM

## INGREDIENTS

4 extra large eggs

1 extra large egg yolk

3–4 tbsp sugar

finely grated zest of 2 medium
    oranges

juice of 3 medium oranges

1¼ pt light cream

pinch of freshly grated nutmeg

2 pinches of ground cinnamon

### FOR THE GARNISH

thinly pared orange peel curled
    into rose shapes

**Serves 4**

Put the whole eggs, the extra yolk and 3 tablespoons of the sugar in a mixing bowl. Whisk until the mixture becomes smooth and pale. Whisk in the orange zest and juice. Gradually stir in the cream, then add the nutmeg and cinnamon. Taste and add more spice and sugar if liked.

Transfer the mixture either to a very heavy saucepan set over very low heat, or to a double-boiler or *bain-marie* set over low to medium heat. Cook gently, stirring constantly with a wooden spoon using a figure-eight motion. When the mixture starts to 'grab' and is thickened enough to coat the spoon thinly, remove from the heat. Stand the base of the pan in iced water or transfer the mixture to a cold dish. Cool the cream, stirring occasionally. If it is not to be served immediately, press plastic wrap over the surface to prevent a skin forming.

Serve the Orange Cream in a bowl or in individual glasses. Decorate with thinly pared orange peel curled into rose shapes.

# SCOTTISH OATCAKES

## INGREDIENTS

2 tbsp unsalted butter, finely diced

1 tsp salt

1⅞ cups fine-ground oatmeal (see
    page 39), or Scotch oats ground
    finely in a food processor

about ⅞ cup boiling water

**Makes 12 to 14**

The traditional way of shaping oatcakes is to press the dough into a round baking pan using the heel of your hand, then to break the whole sheet of oatcake into wedges once it is baked. This takes some practice, and the method I have given in this recipe is easier for the inexperienced oatcake baker.

Put the butter and salt in a small bowl, and put the oatmeal in a larger one. Add the boiling water to the butter and salt. Stir with a whisk and, when the butter has fully melted, pour the mixture over the oatmeal, mixing well. Add a little more boiling water, if necessary, to form a pliable mass. Cover and leave in a cool place overnight. To make the dough easy to roll out, knead it either by hand, or in an electric mixer using the dough hook, until it is pliable without being sticky. Roll it out on a pastry slab or other cold work surface to about ⅛ to ¼ inch thick. Cut it into 3-inch diameter rounds, or triangles, and transfer the shapes to a baking sheet. Cover and leave in a cool place for 1½ hours.

For the best results, bake the oatcakes as slowly as possible. Preheat the oven to 250° and bake for 2½ hours. Alternatively, bake them at 275° for 1½ hours.

Transfer the baked oatcakes to a wire rack and air them well before serving. You can store the oatcakes in an airtight container for several weeks; if you like, reheat them in a very low oven before serving.

# CHUNKY MARMALADE WITH WHISKY

Squeeze the juice from the halved oranges, then strain it to extract the seeds; set the juice and the seeds aside separately. Repeat the process with the lemons.

On a board, cut up the orange peel shells into strips. For a chunky marmalade, cut the strips about ¼ inch wide and about ¾ inch long. Collect any bits of white pith that fall away, then enclose the pith, along with the orange and lemon seeds, in a cheesecloth bag tied with string. Put the strips of orange peel, the cheesecloth bag, orange and lemon juices, water and whisky in a kettle and simmer gently for 2½ hours or until the peel is very soft. Squeeze the cheesecloth bag and remove it.

Add the warmed white and brown sugars and the molasses and stir over gentle heat until the sugar has completely dissolved. Raise the heat and boil rapidly. After 10 minutes, test for setting: either check that the sugar thermometer is registering 220°, or pour a little marmalade on to a chilled plate, let it cool and push with your finger; if the marmalade has formed a skin that will wrinkle, it is ready.

Skim well and allow to cool just until a surface skin forms, then ladle the marmalade into warmed jars, making sure that peel and syrup are evenly distributed. Seal with wax and a cover while the marmalade is still hot. For long storage, process in a boiling water bath (page 17).

## INGREDIENTS

| |
|---|
| 2 lb Seville oranges, washed and halved |
| 2 lemons, halved |
| 4¾ pt water |
| 1 cup Scotch whisky |
| 3 lb (about 7 cups) white sugar, warmed |
| 1 lb (about 2 cups) packed light brown sugar, warmed |
| 3 tbsp molasses |

**Makes about 6 pounds**

# A

## New Orleans

The hallmark of New Orleans food is its flamboyance. This is a city that has established not merely a tolerance of ethnic mixtures but, rather, a regard for them. The French contributed sauces, the Creoles added their seasonings (some of them stingingly hot), the Spanish introduced mixtures of pork, poultry and seafood. The Cajuns, who came down from Canada in 1775, added their own ethnic spices to the melting pot. And, all around, the good American soil yielded a wonderful harvest of exotic fruits and vegetables, with plantains, bananas, sweet potatoes and corn galore.

Some of this spirit is reflected in the brunch menu. The fruit salads that open the meal are certainly on the showy side: the Extravaganza is a ravishing spectacle of tropical fruits contained in a basket carved out of a huge watermelon while the Citrus Sundae offers refreshing orange and grapefruit segments and kiwi fruits, with lime juice, in individual half-grapefruit shells.

Both the main courses combine typical New Orleans produce. The chicken may appear to be a wild confusion of ingredients – sautéed chicken and bananas flambéed in rum, creamed corn arranged in the emptied banana skins and with red peppers scattered throughout the surrounding rice – but the effect is wonderful. Cajun-style Shrimp, with a rich tomato sauce, is in many ways similar to a *jambalaya*, which is a combination of shrimp and rice – often with ham and chicken added as well. But strictly speaking all the ingredients for *jambalaya* should be combined in a single pot, while here the main stew of shrimp and tomatoes is cooked separately from the rice. I prefer this because both flavors and textures remain distinct. Either small brown or large pink shrimps may be used.

The egg dishes on the menu are less striking perhaps, and less evocative of Creole cooking and nineteenth-

CAJUN-STYLE SHRIMP, PECAN PIE

*Selection of Fruit Juice Cocktails,*
*Eye-Openers, Pick-Ups and Punches*

*Watermelon Extravaganza*
*or*
*Citrus Sundae*

*Eggs Florentine*
*or*
*Eggs Benedict*

*Blini*

*New Orleans Chicken*
*with Rice cooked with Sweet Red Peppers*
*or*
*Cajun-style Shrimp in a Spicy Tomato*
*Sauce with Rice*

*Pecan Pie*

*Selection of Breads and Rolls*

*Coffee or Tea*

century Louisiana. 'Florentine' and 'Benedict' belong respectively to Tuscany, and to the United States in general, rather than the Southern states in particular. But many restaurants in New Orleans pride themselves on the scope of their egg dishes. The world-famous Brennan's at 417 Royal Street, for instance, has a vast menu of egg dishes with names like 'Portuguese,' 'Russian,' 'Hussarde,' 'Muenster' and 'à la Nouvelle Orléans.'

So why did I single out, from among the range of unusual-sounding choices, the more obvious Eggs Benedict (recipe on page 59) and Florentine? In part because their ingredients are available throughout most seasons all over the world – consider the difficulty of 'Eggs à la Nouvelle Orleans,' which calls for crab meat and brandy-cream sauce – and partly because, done well, I think they are the best on offer.

They are often done not so well: overcooked eggs and frozen spinach, beneath a floury white sauce finished with an indifferent cheese topping, is a typical rendering of Eggs Florentine. Personally, I do not like cheese anywhere near Eggs Florentine: I prefer a plain white sauce flavored with aromatics, plus a hint of nutmeg.

Delicious as the egg dishes are, they do not flatter a decent wine in the way that Blini with salt fish of some kind most certainly will. My recipe for Blini (page 61) suggests a mixture of buckwheat and plain white flour, rather than the authentic all-buckwheat rendering, which I find too bitter.

The classic Pecan Pie, which finishes the meal, has transcended its cultural origins and become a universal favorite. Another last-minute option for the dessert would be bananas flambéed in rum – provided you are not serving the banana and chicken dish for the main course. This is highly representative of New Orleans cuisine. Simply sauté halved bananas in a mixture of sugar, cinnamon and either banana liqueur or melted clarified butter. Then add some heated rum to the pan and ignite it, tipping and swirling the pan until the flames die out. Serve with whipped cream or vanilla ice cream.

# WATERMELON EXTRAVAGANZA

Watermelon is hollowed out to form a basket and filled with tropical fruits.

To make the watermelon basket, tie a piece of string around the widest part of the watermelon; this will become the rim of the basket. Next, lightly score the handle of the basket. To do this, establish a central point on top of the melon which will become the tallest point of the arched handle. Then, working about 1 inch to the right and left of that point, score two vertical parallel lines, each line running downward to meet the string on both sides. When you have scored the two arcs of the handle, use a large knife to saw vertically down the scored lines to the level of the string. Then, score the melon's circumference marked by the string *except* where it crosses the handle – otherwise you will cut the handle off. Untie the string. Remove the two sections between the handle and the circumference, sawing through the circumference and leaving the handle intact. When the sections are removed, hollow out the flesh from the bottom of the melon to form the basket. Finally, remove the melon flesh from the arc to complete the handle.

Use between one-quarter and half of the melon flesh for the fruit salad; remove the seeds and slice the flesh, then transfer it to a large mixing bowl. Reserve the remaining melon flesh for other preparations and for general eating.

Put the sugar and water into a heavy-based saucepan. Stir over gentle heat until the sugar has dissolved, then raise the heat and bring the syrup to the boil without stirring. Boil the syrup hard for 2 to 3 minutes. Remove from the heat and cool the syrup quickly by setting the base of the pan in iced water.

While the syrup cools, prepare the fruit: peel the mango and papaya; remove the pits or seeds. Cut the fruit into even-sized slices and transfer them to the mixing bowl with the melon. If you are including pineapple, remove its skin, eyes and core, then slice the flesh and add to the bowl. Peel and slice the kiwi fruits and add to the bowl. Cut the passion fruits in half and scoop out their contents, using a small spoon, directly into the bowl.

Pour the cold syrup over the fruit and add a tiny pinch of salt and the lemon juice. Mix everything together very gently, preferably with your hands, so as not to break up the fruit. Arrange the mixture in the watermelon basket. If you wish, add raspberries or strawberries to the arrangement. Place the melon basket on a bed of crushed ice on a large platter, then serve.

## INGREDIENTS

| |
|---|
| 1 large watermelon |
| ½ cup sugar |
| 1½ cups water |
| 1 small ripe mango |
| 1 small ripe papaya |
| ¼ pineapple (optional) |
| 3 kiwi fruits |
| 6 passion fruits |
| pinch of salt |
| juice of ½ lemon |
| 12 raspberries or strawberries (optional) |

**Serves 6**

# CITRUS SUNDAE

## INGREDIENTS

3 large grapefruit, preferably 2
  pink and 1 yellow

3 oranges

pinch of salt

2–4 tbsp sugar

3 firm kiwi fruits

2 limes or small lemons

**Serves 6**

Orange and grapefruit segments, with kiwi fruit and lime juice, are presented here in grapefruit shells.

Cut the grapefruit in half crosswise. Use a serrated knife to remove the segments, and transfer them to a bowl. Scrape the insides of the grapefruit shells clean with a sharp spoon; set them aside.
  Peel the oranges, removing all the white pith. Cut out the segments and add them to the bowl of grapefruit segments. (The best way to do this is to work over the bowl, and peel the oranges with a very sharp knife using a sawing action, turning each orange in one hand. Cut down each side of the dividing membrane so that the segments fall free into the bowl. Finally, squeeze the emptied membrane to extract the juice.) Add a pinch of salt and sugar to taste, and mix all together gently.
  Peel the kiwi fruits and slice them into about 24 slices in all. Spread them out on a large plate. Take three good slices from the limes, cutting from the widest part. Cut these slices in half and reserve them for the garnish. Squeeze the juice from the remaining pieces of lime over the kiwi fruits.
  Arrange the citrus mixture in the grapefruit shells. Add the kiwi slices, distributing them equally. Decorate with the lime slices, nicked and slightly curled.

*Citrus Sundae*

# EGGS FLORENTINE

Poached eggs on a bed of spinach are topped with a nutmeg-flavored classic white sauce.

This recipe demands six poached eggs. It is almost impossible to poach six eggs together; four is about the maximum, even in a wide pan. I poach them in two batches of three. The amount of fresh spinach is based on spinach of medium age, but if you have young, tender leaves, with scarcely any stem, you will need less than the suggested amount.

First make the béchamel sauce: put the flavorings into a saucepan containing the milk. Cover the pan, bring to a gentle simmer over low heat, then set aside in a warm place to infuse for at least 20 minutes. Strain the milk and discard the solids.

Melt the butter in a heavy saucepan set over low heat. Stir in the flour and cook for a few minutes, then raise the heat and pour in the flavored milk, whisking constantly to blend the mixture perfectly smooth as it comes to the boil. Immediately reduce the heat to the lowest setting and leave the sauce to simmer very gently for 30 to 40 minutes, stirring occasionally. Finally, season the sauce well with salt, pepper and nutmeg.

While the sauce is simmering, wash the spinach and remove all tough stems and old leaves. Parboil it in plenty of boiling salted water for about 2 minutes. Drain, refresh under cold water and drain again, squeezing out excess moisture. Chop the spinach and put it into a saucepan containing the butter. Season with salt, pepper and nutmeg, and set aside ready for reheating.

For the eggs, bring a wide shallow pan of water to the boil. Turn off the heat and gently break three of the eggs directly into the water – or break them first into a cup, if you prefer. Cover the pan with a tight-fitting lid and leave the eggs to poach for 3 minutes. Remove them with a slotted spoon and place them in a bowl of warm water. Poach the remaining eggs in the same way and transfer them to the bowl.

Preheat the broiler. Reheat the spinach in the butter, stir in the cream and spread out in a warm gratin dish. Drain the eggs on a towel, trim any ragged edges and arrange them on the bed of spinach. Add the tiniest pinch of salt. Spoon over the sauce and scatter the bread crumbs and slivers of butter on top for a gratin finish. Place the dish beneath the broiler and cook for about 1 ½ minutes or until the surface is lightly colored. Serve directly from the gratin dish.

## INGREDIENTS

6 extra large, very fresh eggs

### FOR THE BECHAMEL SAUCE

flavorings of ½ small onion studded with 4 cloves, about 12 parsley stems, 6 peppercorns, bay leaf and blade of mace

1 ¼ pt milk

3 tbsp unsalted butter

3 tbsp all-purpose flour

salt and freshly ground pepper

freshly grated nutmeg

### FOR THE SPINACH

3 ¼ lb fresh bulk spinach

3 tbsp unsalted butter

½ cup heavy cream

### FOR THE GRATIN FINISH

2 tbsp fine, dry white bread crumbs

½ tbsp unsalted butter

**Serves 6**

*Eggs Florentine*

# NEW ORLEANS CHICKEN

## INGREDIENTS

### FOR THE CHICKEN

6 chicken breast halves, skinned

about 3 tbsp seasoned flour

4 tbsp unsalted butter

2 tbsp olive oil

### FOR THE CORN

4½ cups corn

3 tbsp unsalted butter

¾ cup heavy cream

salt and freshly ground pepper

### FOR THE RICE

2 cups long-grain rice

2 tbsp unsalted butter

1 tbsp oil

1 onion, finely chopped

2 medium-size sweet red peppers,
    cored, seeded and cut into strips

3½ cups chicken or Veal Stock
    (page 32)

### FOR THE BANANAS

6 bananas

½ lemon

small amount of all-purpose flour

1–2 eggs, beaten

2 tbsp unsalted butter

1–2 tbsp white rum

### FOR THE SAUCE

6 tbsp chicken or Veal Stock

⅔ cup white rum

1 cup heavy cream or crème fraîche

2 pinches of cayenne

1 tsp lemon juice

2 small bits of unsalted butter

**Serves 6**

*Opposite: New Orleans Chicken*

This flamboyant dish of tender boned chicken breasts is garnished with rum-flambéed bananas and creamed corn, and is served with rice cooked with sweet red peppers.

Parboil fresh or frozen corn until just tender, then drain. Drain canned corn. Transfer to a saucepan with the butter, cream and seasoning. Cook gently, covered, for about 15 minutes, then keep warm in a covered dish in a very low oven.

While the corn is cooking, prepare the rice. In a large saucepan, heat the butter and oil over a low heat and cook the onion gently. When it has softened slightly, add the sweet red pepper and continue to cook, with the lid on, for a further few minutes. Stir in the rice until the grains are coated with butter, then add the stock or water plus a little salt. Bring to a light boil, uncovered. Stir once, then adjust the heat with the lid set ajar so the liquid simmers. Cook for about 12 minutes or until the liquid is absorbed and the rice is just tender. Transfer to a warm dish, cover the dish with a cloth and place in the oven with the corn.

Lightly coat the chicken breasts with the seasoned flour. Using one large sauté pan, or two smaller ones, heat the butter and oil, then sauté the breasts gently on both sides until just cooked – about 14 minutes for medium-sized breasts. When finished, transfer the breasts to a warm dish, cover with foil and keep warm in the oven. Reserve the pan(s) without washing.

While the chicken is cooking, prepare the bananas. Lay the bananas in their skins on the work surface and cut them in half lengthwise. Slip the bananas out of their skins. Rub the insides of the skins with half a cut lemon; set them aside. Roll the banana halves gently in a little flour, then in beaten egg. Sauté the bananas in butter in a clean frying pan until lightly browned, starting on the rounded side of the fruit, then turning the fruit over. Drain off excess fat and flambé the bananas with the rum. Keep the bananas warm in a covered dish.

Pour off all excess fat from the pan in which the chicken was cooked, leaving only the sediment behind. (If you are using only one pan, you will need slightly less than the quantities given to make the sauce.) Set the pan over medium heat and, when hot, add the stock and rum. Scrape the crusty sediment from the pan and incorporate it into the liquid. Add the cream and lightly boil the sauce until it reduces by about half. Season to taste, adding the cayenne and lemon juice. Keep warm.

Arrange the chicken breasts on the rice on a large flat serving platter. Fill the half-banana skins with the corn mixture and top with a sautéed banana half. Off the heat, whisk the butter into the sauce, and spoon a little of it over the chicken breasts; serve the remainder separately. If you like, garnish with sprigs of fresh coriander (cilantro) and serve.

# CAJUN-STYLE SHRIMP
## IN A SPICY TOMATO SAUCE

### INGREDIENTS

2¼ lb cooked medium-size shrimp in shell, or 18 oz cooked small shrimp in shell

2 cups long-grain rice

2 small or 1½ large green bell peppers, cored, seeded and diced

3 tbsp finely chopped fresh parsley

### FOR THE TOMATO SAUCE

2 tbsp unsalted butter

3–4 tbsp olive oil

3 medium-size onions, finely chopped

3 large garlic cloves, finely chopped

3½ lb ripe tomatoes, peeled, cored and seeded, or 3 × 1-lb cans whole tomatoes, drained

3 large sprigs fresh thyme

3 bay leaves

2 tsp dried oregano

1 tsp allspice berries, crushed

¾ cup red wine

salt and freshly ground pepper

1–2 tsp sugar

1 tsp Tabasco sauce

¼ tsp hot chili powder

### FOR THE GARNISH

6 cooked jumbo shrimp in shell

6 wedges of lemon

**Serves 6**

The bonus of this dish is that its base of tomato sauce is simple to make and can be prepared well in advance, as can the rice. Then, when guests are looking hungry, you can bring the sauce briefly to a simmer, add the shrimp and green peppers and serve the whole thing minutes later. The sauce can be as spicy as you like, or not at all. In fact, if you omit the hot, tingling seasonings of chili and Tabasco, you have a tomato sauce with a delightful, fresh taste overlaid with the mildly aromatic flavors of oregano, bay and thyme. If available, crayfish make an excellent alternative to the shrimp.

First make the tomato sauce. In a large, heavy-based saucepan, gently heat the butter and oil and sweat the onions until soft but not brown. Stir in the garlic and, after a few minutes, add the tomatoes, herbs, allspice and wine. Bring to a light boil, stirring, then adjust the heat to maintain a brisk simmer and cook uncovered for 30 to 40 minutes, adding only the tiniest pinch of salt toward the end.

While the sauce simmers, peel the shrimp. (If you are using small shrimp, top and tail them.) You can either prepare the rice now and keep it warm – wrapped in cheesecloth in a steamer or covered with a cloth in a very low oven – or you can cook it later, when the sauce is almost ready.

Press the tomato sauce through a nylon sieve and discard the solids, or pass it through the finest blade of a food mill, first picking out the sprigs of thyme and bay. Return the sauce to a clean pan and reduce it further if necessary – it should coat the spoon like heavy cream. Taste and check the seasoning, adding the sugar if necessary, plus salt and pepper. To give the sauce a hot, Cajun-style flavor, add the Tabasco and chili powder. Add the green pepper and shrimp to the sauce. Over gentle heat, return the sauce to a simmer and maintain it gently for about 5 minutes, taking care not to overcook and toughen the shrimp. Stir in the parsley, then turn the mixture out on to a warm serving dish, along with the rice. Decorate with the whole jumbo shrimp and lemon wedges, and serve.

# PECAN PIE

As a variation of traditional pecan pie, a rich filling of pecans and maple syrup is set in an orange and cinnamon-flavored crust.

To make the pastry, sift the flour, sugar and salt into a large mixing bowl. Stir in the cinnamon. Add the butter and rub or cut it into the flour until large crumbs form. Add the orange zest. Distribute the egg yolk mixture over the top and stir briskly with a fork to blend. Gather up the dough into a ball, adding a drop or two more milk if the dough does not adhere. Press it together, wrap and chill it for 15 minutes.

Roll out the dough evenly and line a 9-inch flan or quiche dish. (If the dish has a loose bottom, make doubly sure that the covering of dough is even, so as to prevent any seepage.) Prick the dough lightly, cover with foil and chill for at least 15 minutes.

Preheat the oven to 400°. Bake the pastry case for 15 minutes. Remove the foil and bake for a further 5 minutes. Set aside.

To make the filling, lightly beat the eggs, then add the sifted sugar and salt and beat until smooth. Beat in the syrup, rum and cream. Chop about half of the nuts and put them in the pastry case, then arrange the remaining pecan halves on top of the chopped nuts. Pour over the filling mixture. Protect the edges of the crust with a rim of foil.

Reduce the oven temperature to 350° and bake the pie for about 35 minutes, removing the foil protection toward the end of cooking. Serve the pie warm, either with chilled whipped cream or with vanilla ice cream.

## INGREDIENTS

### FOR THE PASTRY

| |
|---|
| 1 ¼ cups all-purpose flour |
| 2 tsp sugar |
| ¼ tsp salt |
| ½ tsp ground cinnamon |
| 6 tbsp cold unsalted butter, finely diced |
| finely grated zest of ½ orange |
| 1 egg yolk, beaten with 3½ tbsp milk |

### FOR THE FILLING

| |
|---|
| 3 extra large eggs |
| ½ cup light brown sugar |
| pinch of salt |
| ½ cup maple syrup |
| 2 tbsp light rum |
| 2 tbsp heavy cream |
| about 1 ¾ cups pecan halves |

**Serves 6**

*Cajun-style Shrimp*

# 'Have a nice day'

## BREAKFAST USA

It is easy to understand the popularity of breakfast in American restaurants: the ingredients are good and, generally speaking, there is no attempt to deceive the breakfaster – for example, fresh orange juice is fresh and not from a concentrate. Most of all, the choice is enormous. The toast and fruit dishes alone can treble all items listed on a breakfast menu in any other part of the world. Choosing what to have for breakfast can be a positive challenge, especially to a mind only half awake.

I remember my first American breakfast. It was in New York, and I was still a trifle jet-lagged. Ordering was an ordeal. After I meekly announced each choice – fruit juice, eggs, toast, coffee and so on – the waiter automatically repeated, robot-fashion, the words 'What kind of . . .?' Frankly, my brain hurt.

After that I rapidly learned what all the different 'kinds' were, and got quite good at racing explicitly through the menu specifying how I wanted my eggs (over easy), my bacon (thinly sliced, slightly smoked, sweet-cure Canadian, broiled crisp), my crushed pineapple juice (with ice) and so on, without any queries coming back at me. In fact, it became a daily litmus test for alertness, rather like doing *The Times* crossword. If I didn't get a single 'What kind of. . .?' from the waiter, I reckoned I really *was* going to have that nice day everyone kept wishing me.

Just when I thought I'd got the hang of it, I found myself in Honolulu. Stupidly, I didn't pick up the menu, and ordered instead straight off my head. All went well until the Cinnamon Toast. Just as I got the words out, the waiter was there with 'What kind of. . .?' What options could there be? My brain started to hurt again. The options turned out to be a choice of 14 types of bread; whether to have it toasted on one side or two; then whether to have the cinnamon and sugar mixed and put

*Sunrise Supreme*
*or*
*Baked Apple*
*with a Walnut-Butterscotch Sauce*
*or*
*Banana Flip*

*Eggs Benedict*
*or*
*Oyster Omelette*
*or*
*A Selection of Egg Dishes, including*
*Over Easy and Sunny Side Up*

*Blini or Waffles or Bagels*

*Blueberry Muffins*
*or*
*Cinnamon Toast*
*or*
*Selection of Breads and Rolls*

*Coffee or Tea*

on the toast, then the toast returned to the broiler to melt the sugar; or whether to have the cinnamon and sugar brought separately to the table so that I could blend it to my own liking. Finally, I made my choice and the waiter scurried off.

At this point I threw a nervous 'well-whatever-next?' smile at the adjoining table, where a prosperous-looking middle-aged man was contentedly tipping all manner of jams over his bacon and waffles. 'This mulberry jelly's not like Bessie makes back home,' he said wistfully. 'Wish I'd settled for the Mexican corn bread, with the Sloppy Joe topping.' His wife retorted, 'Should have had the Strawberries Suzette with the waffles like I told you. They sure are great with these pineapple fritters and ice cream.' She was probably right.

There couldn't be an American breakfast without Eggs Benedict – that renowned assembly of ham or bacon on a buttery muffin, with a lightly poached egg on top, and the whole thing snuggled beneath a velvety blanket of hollandaise sauce. It is a simple enough concept. But to execute it to perfection, you unfortunately need two pairs of hands: one pair to poach the eggs; the other pair to whisk butter into the hollandaise. The brutal facts are that poached eggs require vigilance, and are at their best when eaten almost straight out of their poaching water – after draining and trimming, that is; left for any length of time, they become either cold or hard, or both. And as for hollandaise, it is at its smooth, elegant best when the last bit of butter has been whisked into it; after that, it is likely to become a scruffy rebel, and to fall apart or thicken if left for any length of time.

This recipe is geared for the one-pair-of-hands-home-cook, with no helper in the kitchen. I start the hollandaise and continue until about half the butter has been incorporated. Then I set it aside briefly while I poach the eggs and transfer them to warm water. I quickly complete the hollandaise, whisking in the remaining butter while the eggs are, simultaneously, being kept warm for the minimum length of time.

# SUNRISE SUPREME

Pieces of apple, grapefruit and melon are served very attractively in a half-melon shell on a bed of ice.

Cut the melons in half and discard the seeds. If necessary, take a very thin slice off the curved bottom of each melon half so that it will stand up securely. Run the tip of a small, sharp knife around the cut surface of each half about ½ inch from the outside edge. Then slice downward along this line to remove the flesh in four or five sections, each about 1 ½ inches wide at their widest part. Cut across the sections to give fan-shaped slices and set them aside in a bowl. (Alternatively, use a melon baller to remove and shape the flesh into little balls.) Set the melon shells aside.

Peel the grapefruit and divide it into membrane-free segments as you would an orange (see page 48). Put the segments into the bowl with the melon flesh and squeeze over the juice from the grapefruit membrane.

Quarter and core the apple (leave the peel on if you wish), then cut it into fan-shaped slices. Turn the slices in the lemon juice to prevent them discoloring, then amalgamate with the melon and grapefruit.

Arrange the fruit mixture in the melon shells and sit them on a bed of crushed ice. If you like, decorate each with a strawberry or with a purée of strawberries.

## INGREDIENTS

| |
|---|
| 2 cantaloupe melons, each weighing about 1 ¾ lb |
| 1 grapefruit, preferably pink |
| 1 crisp medium-size apple |
| juice of 1 lemon |

FOR THE GARNISH
(OPTIONAL)

| |
|---|
| 4 large strawberries, or about 1 cup strawberry purée |

**Serves 4**

*Sunrise Supreme*

# BAKED APPLE
## WITH A WALNUT-BUTTERSCOTCH SAUCE

### INGREDIENTS

4 large firm-textured apples, such as Granny Smith

4 tsp liquid honey

2 tbsp raisins

1 tbsp chopped walnuts

2 tbsp chopped dried apricots

about 2 tbsp unsalted butter

about ⅔ cup white wine or water

### FOR THE SAUCE

2 tbsp light corn syrup

1 tbsp light brown sugar

½ tbsp unsalted butter

4 tbsp water

6 tbsp heavy cream or crème fraîche

½ tsp lemon juice

2 tbsp coarsely chopped walnuts

**Serves 4**

Baked apples are delicious on their own and do not beg an accompaniment, but there is no doubt that the Walnut-Butterscotch Sauce elevates them into something special.

Preheat the oven to 350°.

Lightly score the apples around their middles so that the skins will not burst during cooking. Partially core the apples, starting at the wider, stem end, and taking care to leave the apple intact at the opposite end so that the filling can be contained.

Fill the apples with the honey, raisins, walnuts and apricots, adding the ingredients a little at a time and in layers. Finish with a dot of butter. Arrange the apples to fit snugly in a shallow baking dish, then pour around the wine or water. Bake for about 30 minutes or until the apples are tender but still retain their shape; baste occasionally. Remove from the oven and allow to cool slightly before serving with Walnut-Butterscotch Sauce, or cream.

Toward the end of the apples' cooking time, make the Walnut-Butterscotch Sauce. Put the syrup, sugar and butter in a small heavy-based saucepan. Set over low heat and stir with a wooden spoon until the sugar has dissolved, then raise the heat slightly and continue to cook, stirring, until the mixture is smooth and fairly thick. Add the water, bring to the boil and boil for about 3 minutes.

Stir in the cream, return to the boil and boil for a further 2 minutes. Add the lemon juice and walnuts, stir over gentle heat for another minute or so, then serve.

# BANANA FLIP

### INGREDIENTS

juice of ½ lemon

about 1 cup heavy cream

2 tbsp liquid honey

4 bananas

### FOR THE GARNISH

few pinches of ground cinnamon

4 slices of lemon

8 sprigs of mint

**Serves 4**

This pretty assembly consists of bananas with a lemon and honey-flavored cream, finished with cinnamon and garnished with fresh mint.

Put the lemon juice in a mixing bowl. Beat in the cream gradually, adding only a little at a time. When just over half the cream has been added, the mixture will 'grab' and thicken. Continue to add the cream and, finally, stir in the honey.

Peel the bananas and slice them in half lengthwise. Arrange two banana halves, flat-side down, on each of four serving plates. Spoon over the cream, making patterns with the back of the spoon. Sprinkle over the cinnamon and decorate with the slices of lemon and the mint.

# EGGS BENEDICT

Split each muffin in half, and trim the slices of ham to fit. Set the muffins and ham aside.

To start the hollandaise sauce, put the vinegar and water mixture into a small, heavy saucepan and boil down until reduced to 1 tablespoon. Meanwhile, bring a wide, shallow pan of water to a simmer, so that it is conveniently ready to poach the eggs at a later stage.

Transfer the vinegar and water reduction to a bowl. Add ½ tablespoon of cold water, then add the egg yolks and whisk until smooth. Suspend the bowl over a pan of simmering water to form a *bain-marie* (the bottom of the bowl should not touch the water). Continue to whisk for a moment or two, then gradually whisk in about half of the butter, in tiny batches, introducing a new batch only when the previous one has been absorbed, and whisking all the time. At this stage, the hollandaise will be half-prepared, ready to be completed once the eggs have been poached.

Remove the *bain-marie* from the heat while you poach the eggs in the pan of simmering water (see page 15). Remove each egg with a slotted spoon after about 3 minutes of cooking, then trim the edges and transfer to a bowl of warm water.

Complete the hollandaise sauce by replacing the *bain-marie* over heat and whisking in the remaining butter as before. Season to taste, and add a little lemon juice. Remove the sauce from the *bain-marie* and set aside.

Toast the muffin halves, spread with butter and arrange on plates. Cover with the ham and add a poached egg, first drained on a cloth. Top with the hollandaise sauce. If you like, serve with extra toasted muffins and a garnish of watercress. Tomato and lemon are other garnish possibilities.

### INGREDIENTS

| |
|---|
| 4 extra large, very fresh eggs |
| 4 slices of cooked ham, weighing about ¼ lb in total, trimmed of fat |
| 2 English muffins, plus unsalted butter for spreading |

### FOR THE HOLLANDAISE SAUCE

| |
|---|
| 3 tbsp tarragon or wine vinegar mixed with 2 tbsp cold water |
| 3 extra large egg yolks |
| 7 oz (1¾ sticks) cold unsalted butter, finely diced |
| salt and freshly ground pepper |
| about ½ tsp lemon juice |

### FOR THE GARNISH (OPTIONAL)

| |
|---|
| watercress |

**Serves 4**

# OYSTER OMELETTE

## INGREDIENTS

4 small to medium-size oysters, shells opened and oysters loosened

few drops of lemon juice

2 extra large eggs

1 tbsp cold unsalted butter, finely diced

salt and freshly ground pepper

small bit of butter for cooking the omelette

1 tsp finely chopped fresh parsley

### FOR THE GARNISH

small wedge of lemon

parsley

**Serves 1**

*Oyster Omelette*

Oysters must be fresh. To open them use an oyster knife. Hold the oyster with its shell flat side uppermost, wrapped in a cloth to prevent slipping and to protect your hand. Insert the knife blade under the hinge and twist the blade to separate the shells. Slide the blade along the shell to sever the muscle.

Slide three of the oysters complete with their juices into a small pan and add the lemon juice. Cook over low to medium heat, turning once, for about 1 minute or until the edges curl. Set the oysters aside in a warm place.

Break the eggs into a shallow dish. Add the diced butter, a relatively small amount of salt, for the oysters will provide some of their own, and pepper to taste. Heat a 7-inch omelette pan, adding a small bit of butter to it. While the butter melts, beat the egg mixture lightly with a fork. When the butter in the pan starts to foam, tip in the egg mixture. Cook the omelette in the normal way, tilting the pan and passing the flat of a fork through the mixture so that any uncooked egg can make contact with a hot surface. Add the parsley and the oysters – transferred with a slotted spoon to reserve their juices.

Roll up the omelette, seal and tip on to a warm plate. Drizzle the oyster juices over the omelette. Garnish with the remaining oyster on its half shell, a small wedge of lemon and a sprig of parsley, whole or chopped.

# BLINI

These blini are made with a mixture of buckwheat and white wheat flours, but they may also be made entirely with buckwheat flour or entirely with white wheat flour. The buckwheat version has a marked bitter taste, the other a sweet one.

In a large, warmed bowl, dissolve the yeast in only a little of the warm water, mixing to a smooth paste. Gradually add the remaining warm water along with all the buckwheat flour and about one-fifth of the white flour, stirring until thoroughly blended. Cover the bowl with a cloth and leave to rise in a warm place for about 30 minutes, or until the yeast batter has doubled in bulk.

Beat in the remaining white flour and, when smooth, beat in the melted butter, egg yolk, salt and sugar. Gradually add the warm milk, stirring to achieve a well-blended mixture. Cover and leave to rise in a warm place for about 40 minutes, or until the mixture appears bubbly.

Beat the egg white to soft peaks, then fold it into the mixture, blending gently to ensure that no pockets of beaten white remain. Cover and leave to rise in a warm place for about 1 hour.

Brush a small, heavy-based frying pan with melted clarified butter or with oil, and set it over medium heat. When the pan is hot, pour a small quantity of the mixture – about half a demi-tasse coffee cup, or about 3 tablespoons – into the pan. The blini should spread to about 4 ½ inches in diameter. Cook for several minutes on each side. Transfer to a warm dish, and repeat the procedure until all the mixture has been used.

Serve the blini with caviar and sour cream, or with cream cheese, or salted herring. Other alternatives include melted butter, *fromage frais* and jam.

## INGREDIENTS

| |
|---|
| 2 tsp active dry yeast |
| 1 cup lukewarm water |
| ¾ cup buckwheat flour |
| 1 cup all-purpose flour |
| 1 ½ tbsp melted butter |
| 1 extra large egg, separated |
| ¼ tsp salt |
| 1 ½ tbsp sugar |
| 1 cup lukewarm milk |
| little oil or melted clarified butter for cooking |

**Makes 20 blini about 4 ½ inches in diameter**

# WAFFLES

## INGREDIENTS

1⅔ cups all-purpose flour

1 tsp baking powder

¼ tsp salt

2–3 tbsp sugar (optional)

2 extra large eggs, separated

1½ cups milk

1 tsp finely grated lemon zest

1 tsp finely grated orange zest

1 tbsp liqueur such as Grand
   Marnier or Cointreau or rum
   (optional)

4 tbsp butter, melted and cooled

clarified butter or sunflower oil for
   cooking

**Makes 12 small waffles**

Sift the flour, baking powder, salt and sugar – if you are including it – into a bowl. Make a well in the center. Beat the egg yolks into the milk, then pour into the well and use a whisk to stir the liquid into the flour mixture. Stir in the zest and, if you like, liqueur. Add the melted butter and stir smooth without overbeating. Cover and set aside for about 30 minutes – or up to 3 hours if it is more convenient.

Heat the waffle iron gently but thoroughly on each side. Meanwhile, beat the egg whites to soft, medium peaks and fold them into the waffle batter until well blended. Grease the grid of the iron evenly and thoroughly with either clarified butter or with sunflower oil (unless using a nonstick waffle iron).

Just cover the grid with batter, then close the iron. If using an electric waffle iron, cook until the waffle stops steaming and both sides of the waffle are golden brown. For a hand-held waffle iron, cook for about 1 minute, then open the lid and check that the waffle is set and the underside pale brown. Turn and cook for 1 to 3 minutes on the other side or until the waffle is cooked to your liking. Transfer the waffle to a baking sheet and keep hot in a very low oven. Repeat the process, greasing the iron between cooking each waffle. Serve with bacon and/or maple syrup. Alternatively you may serve waffles with almost any manner of cream, such as sweetened whipped cream or ice cream, and fruit. Purées of strawberries and raspberries are particularly good.

# BAGELS

In a small bowl, dissolve the sugar in about half of the milk. Add the yeast, then whisk. Cover and set aside in a warm place for about 15 minutes or until the mixture foams slightly.

Sift the flour and salt into a large bowl. Make a well in the center and add the melted butter, the yeast mixture and the remaining milk. Mix well, gradually drawing in the flour from the sides. Knead the dough well on a lightly floured surface until smooth and elastic. Return to a clean bowl, cover and leave to rise in a warm place for about 1 hour, or until doubled in bulk.

On a lightly floured surface, divide the dough into about 12 equal pieces. Shape each piece into a ring with a hole in the middle. You can do this in two ways: either roll each piece of dough into a rope, then join up the ends to form a ring; or shape the dough into a ball, poke a hole in the middle with your finger and enlarge the hole. Once you have shaped the bagels, arrange them on a dish or tray. Cover and leave to rise in a warm place for about 20 minutes. Meanwhile, prepare a greased baking sheet and set a large pan of water to boil. Preheat the oven to 400°.

Transfer the bagels, in batches of about five, to the boiling water, adjusting the heat to maintain a simmer. The bagels will sink at first, then rise to the surface and expand. Count about 8 minutes poaching time. Remove the bagels with a slotted spoon and drain on a towel or rack.

Arrange the poached and drained bagels on the greased baking sheet. Brush the surface with the egg yolk glaze and, if you like, add sesame seeds or sea salt. Bake for 15 to 20 minutes or until light golden brown. The bagels are at their best served warm. Offer cream cheese and smoked salmon (lox) as an accompaniment; or you could replace the cream cheese with sour cream.

## INGREDIENTS

| |
|---|
| 2 tbsp sugar |
| ⅞ cup lukewarm milk |
| 2 tsp active dry yeast |
| 2⅓ cups bread flour |
| 1 tsp salt |
| 4 tbsp unsalted butter, melted and cooled |
| 1 egg yolk mixed with 1 tsp cold water, for the glaze |
| about 1 tbsp sesame seeds, or 2 tsp sea or kosher salt |

**Makes about 12**

*Bagels, Quick Bran and Raisin Muffins*

# BLUEBERRY MUFFINS

## INGREDIENTS

1⅔ cups bread flour

2 tsp baking powder

½ tsp salt

¼ cup sugar

2 extra large eggs, beaten

5 tbsp unsalted butter, melted

about ¾ cup milk

finely grated zest of ½ small
    lemon

finely grated zest of ½ small
    orange

1¼ cups blueberries, lightly
    floured

**Makes 12**

Butter the muffin pans well; set aside. Preheat the oven to 400°

Sift the flour, baking powder, salt and sugar into a large bowl. Make a well in the center and add the eggs, butter and most of the milk. Stir with a fork. Add the fruit zests and the blueberries, then stir once or twice again very quickly and briefly, so as not to overbeat the batter. If the batter is still firm, gently stir in the remaining milk.

Spoon the batter into the cups in the muffin pans, and place immediately in the oven. After a minute or two, lower the oven temperature to 375° and bake the muffins for 25 to 35 minutes or until risen.

Transfer the muffins to a rack and allow to cool slightly. Serve them, whole, in a napkin with butter and cream. The traditional way to eat muffins is to pull them apart, as opposed to cutting them in half.

Cranberries, red currants, dried fruit and chopped nuts are all alternatives to blueberries.

# CINNAMON TOAST

## INGREDIENTS

2 tsp ground cinnamon

4 tsp sugar

4 large slices bread, crusts removed

butter for spreading

**Serves 4**

Mix the cinnamon and sugar together; set aside. Toast the bread on both sides under the broiler. Butter generously on one side, then sprinkle with the cinnamon mixture. Place beneath the broiler just long enough to melt the sugar. Serve hot.

*Opposite: Blueberry Muffins*

# A

## Barbecue

### B R U N C H

There is something very appealing about cooking food over glowing embers just as it was cooked centuries ago, when the term barbecue referred to whole, mighty beasts being spitted from '*barbe à queue*' (beard to tail) before being roasted over smoldering wood. The term may well have been coined by the early French huntsmen who settled in America.

I have avoided whole beasts, both small and mighty, and even certain robust-looking bits of them, such as leg of lamb and steaks. This is largely because I have tried to draw a line between what is suitable for brunch as opposed to lunch – although necessarily the line is an arbitrary one, since eating habits are a matter of personal temperament. Speaking for myself, I know that if I have risen late, skipped breakfast and moved straight on to brunch, then I cannot face large pieces of meat for my first meal of the day. I imagine that most people who can will already have their favorite way of preparing such cuts.

Many of the dishes use the natural attributes of ingredients to provide protection from scorching or burning. The Turkey and Shrimp Brochettes and the Noisettes of Lamb are marinated, the first in cream and the second in yogurt, plus an acidic element such as lemon juice, herbs and seasoning. These marinades are used later to baste the food and to protect it from direct heat as it cooks. Of course, they also lend flavor and the acidic element tenderizes the meat. Note that they do not contain oil, which needs caution and vigilance when it comes to barbecues; if it drips on to the hot coals, it can cause sudden flares which scorch the food. If, nevertheless, you prefer an oil-based marinade, try the one scented with a classic persillade of parsley, lemon, garlic and thyme that I give as an alternative on page 75.

Breakfast on a Stick is what you might imagine: a

# TURKEY AND SHRIMP BROCHETTES, TOMATO AND SWEET PEPPER SAUCE, ORANGES IN THE ASHES

*Selection of Eye-Openers, Pick-Ups
and Punches*

*Zucchini Packages
or
Grilled Corn with Parsley Butter*

*Breakfast on a Stick
Tomato and
Sweet Pepper Sauce
or
Whole Calf's Liver Wrapped in Caul,
Mushroom Caps Filled with Chervil
Butter
or
Turkey and Shrimp Brochettes,
Saffron Rice
or
Noisettes of Lamb
Marinated in Mint and Yogurt*

*Pineapple and Orange Brochettes with
a Strawberry Coulis
or
Oranges in the Ashes*

brochette of bacon, kidney, sausage and tomato – ordinary, tasty, appetizing fare. It can be enlivened with the spicy Tomato and Sweet Pepper Sauce; Saffron Rice will transform it into something more substantial and colorful.

The sauce is highly versatile. Delicious with a wide range of simple meat and poultry dishes, such as pork chops, lamb kebabs, steaks, hamburgers and broiled or rotisseried chicken, it also goes well with fish, most notably grey mullet, sea bass and swordfish steaks, and is a good companion to the Turkey and Shrimp Brochettes.

The Grilled Corn with Parsley Butter makes an excellent first course for the Turkey and Shrimp Brochettes.

Ingredients with skins are also ideal for the barbecue. An alternative main course, though no recipe is given, might be duck breasts with mango. You simply cook the ingredients until done to your liking; the skins of both duck and mango provide a shield from the heat.

Calf's Liver Wrapped in Caul is simple but excellent; the lacy shawl of caul bastes the liver as it cooks to pink, juicy succulence. Mushrooms are perfect with the liver – either the Mushroom Caps Filled with Chervil Butter from this menu, or a Mushroom Purée (page 83). The purée could also be matched to simple barbecued chicken or hamburgers.

The Zucchini Packages with tomato and oregano provide a contrast of color and texture, and can be served not only as a first course (a good choice before the liver, for example) but also as an accompaniment to the Noisettes of Lamb – or simple main courses, such as steaks, chops and spit roasts, which do not involve a sauce containing either tomato or zucchini.

The desserts employ the barbecue in different ways: the Pineapple and Orange Brochettes are cooked directly over the coals, whereas foil-wrapped, baked oranges are buried in hot ashes. Try also pitted peaches, crumbled macaroons and a splash of brandy, all wrapped up in foil, then placed on the grill. If you plan to start the brunch early – that is, before noon – you could serve these not as desserts but, rather, as first courses, the offering of fruit to open the meal being more within the strict traditions of breakfast.

# ZUCCHINI PACKAGES

Loosen the skins of the tomatoes by plunging them briefly into hot water, then into cold. Skin and core the tomatoes. Cut three of them vertically into thin slices; set the slices aside. Halve the remaining tomatoes horizontally, scoop out and discard the seeds, then chop the flesh finely and set aside. Have ready six squares of foil, greased with a little of the olive oil.

On a wooden board, cut each zucchini in half lengthwise. Lay the halves cut-side down and, starting at the tip end of each half, as opposed to its stem end, cut ¼-inch thick slices lengthwise. Stop within ½ inch of the stem, thus leaving the slices attached.

Carefully transfer each zucchini half to a square of oiled foil. Spread out the slices slightly to form a fan, and put a slice or two of tomato between each section. Season well with salt and pepper. Season the chopped tomato and add about 1 table-spoon of it to each package. Sprinkle over the oregano. Finally, add a drizzle of oil and 1 tablespoon of white wine to each package. Close the packages.

Set the packages on the barbecue grill, over medium-hot coals, and cook for 20 to 25 minutes, turning once. Unwrap the packages and slide the contents on to serving plates. Serve hot.

## INGREDIENTS

| |
|---|
| 5 large tomatoes |
| about 7 tbsp olive oil |
| 3 large zucchini, weighing about 1 lb in total, washed and trimmed |
| salt and freshly ground pepper |
| 2 tbsp dried oregano |
| 6 tbsp dry white wine |

**Serves 6**

## BARBECUE TIPS

*   Light your barbecue well in advance – as a rough guide, at least one hour ahead of cooking. What you want is smoldering embers – not flames. Get to know how long it takes to achieve the desired effect, depending on the style of barbecue and type of fuel being used.
*   Charcoal briquettes produce a longer-lasting heat – and a more even one – then lump charcoal.
*   Arrange the charcoal in a mound and, once it is lit, leave it to burn undisturbed until the flames have died down and a fine white ash appears on the coals—40-60 minutes. Then, spread the coals out slightly to make a single layer.
*   To replendish the heat source, add more charcoal round the edges.
*   The addition of fruit wood, vine cuttings and herbs to the heat source imparts an aromatic overlay of flavor to the food.
*   To lend lamb, chicken and fish the flavor of rosemary, use a long branch of rosemary as a basting brush.

*Testing the heat*
It is important to be able to gauge the heat of the coals. There is a straightforward, albeit rather primitive, heat test: hold your hand some 5 inches from the heat source. If you can count to five before your hand feels uncomfortably hot, then the coals have low heat. If you can only count to two or three, then the heat is lively, and the coals medium-hot. If you can scarcely count to two, the coals are very hot indeed.

# GRILLED CORN
## WITH PARSLEY BUTTER

### INGREDIENTS

1 ½ sticks unsalted butter, at room
  temperature

3 tbsp finely chopped fresh parsley

salt and freshly ground pepper

6 ears young corn, complete with
  husks and silk

**Serves 6**

Work the butter with a fork and incorporate the parsley and seasoning. Form it into little balls or pats, and set them aside in the refrigerator.

Taking one ear of corn at a time, carefully unfold the strips of green leafy husk and peel them downwards as far as the base. Remove and discard all the silky threads. Fold back the sections of husk to their original position, and tie a small piece of string around the tip to hold them in place.

About 10 to 15 minutes before you want to cook the corn, put it to soak in cold water. This ensures that the corn remains moist during cooking. Then drain it in a colander without patting it dry, so that the ears remain damp.

Place the ears on the oiled barbecue grill, set about 4 to 6 inches above medium-hot coals, and cook, turning the corn frequently, for about 15 minutes or until the husks are dark brown on all sides. If it is more convenient, you can keep the ears warm for 10 minutes or so before serving by pushing them to the coolest part of the barbecue, or by placing them in a very low oven.

When ready to serve, cut and discard the strings, then peel back a section of the husk. Spread the corn with the parsley butter, and have extra butter to hand in case guests wish to help themselves to more.

*Breakfast on a Stick*

# BREAKFAST ON A STICK

You could add small pieces of calf's liver or button mushrooms to these brochettes.

Remove excess fat and surrounding membrane from the kidneys. Cut them in half and remove the core. Season with salt and brush with oil. Cut each slice of bacon, crosswise, into three pieces, then roll up each piece.

Lightly oil six long skewers, and thread each one alternately with sausage, tomato, bacon, kidney and so on, finishing with a tomato. Brush well with oil. Grind over pepper.

Place the brochettes on the barbecue grill, set over medium-hot coals, and cook for 5 to 7 minutes on each side. Transfer to a heated serving dish, and garnish with watercress. Drizzle a little Tomato and Sweet Pepper Sauce (see below) over the brochettes, and serve the remaining sauce separately.

## INGREDIENTS

6 lambs' kidneys

salt and freshly ground pepper

about 3 tbsp olive oil

6 slices bacon

18 small 'cocktail' pork link sausages, or 6 ordinary pork link sausages, each cut crosswise into 3

18 cherry tomatoes, washed

### FOR SERVING

watercress

Tomato and Sweet Pepper Sauce

**Serves 6**

# TOMATO AND SWEET PEPPER SAUCE

Drain off any excess watery liquid from the canned tomatoes, then tip them into a nylon strainer set over a bowl. With a wooden spoon, push the tomatoes and juice through the strainer to make a thin purée. Discard the seeds and solids in the strainer. Set the purée aside.

Heat the oil gently in a heavy-based saucepan and sweat the onion until soft but not colored. Add the garlic and green pepper and stir for 1 to 2 minutes, then add the chilis, tomato purée, chili powder, sugar, mustard and lemon juice. Bring to a vigorous boil, uncovered, then adjust the heat to maintain a light boil and leave to cook for 20 to 30 minutes, stirring occasionally.

Taste the sauce and season. Continue to simmer until the sauce reaches a consistency that will coat the spoon. Use immediately or remove from the heat and reheat – on the barbecue, if liked – at a later stage. Just before serving, stir in the parsley.

## INGREDIENTS

4 × 16 oz cans tomatoes

1/3 cup olive oil

1 large onion, finely chopped

1 fat garlic clove, finely chopped

1 sweet green pepper, cored, seeded and cut into small pieces

1–2 green chili peppers, weighing about 1 oz in total, seeded and finely chopped

1/4 tsp hot chili powder

1 tbsp sugar

2 tsp prepared English (hot) mustard

2 tsp lemon juice

salt and freshly ground pepper

3 tbsp finely chopped fresh parsley

**Serves 6**

# WHOLE CALF'S LIVER
## WRAPPED IN CAUL

### INGREDIENTS

*a piece of caul (membrane of a pig's stomach), large enough to enclose the liver*

*1 whole calf's liver, weighing about 1 ½ lb*

*salt*

*few pinches of dried sage (optional)*

*about 4 tbsp olive oil*

*freshly ground pepper*

### FOR THE GARNISH

*wedges of lemon*

*watercress*

**Serves 8**

*Whole Calf's Liver Wrapped in Caul*

You may have to order the caul and liver in advance from your butcher. Ideally the caul should be fresh rather than salt-dried.

With the cooking times I have given, the liver will appear extremely rare when it comes off the barbecue grill; but after the resting period in a warm place, the blood-tinged juices will distribute themselves throughout the liver and become reabsorbed as the liver cooks a little more in its own heat.

If the caul has been salt-dried, soak it in cold water for 20 minutes, changing the water once or twice, or until all traces of salt have gone. Drain the caul well and pat it absolutely dry.

Peel away the surface membrane from the liver. Sprinkle the liver with salt and, if you like, a little dried sage, then wrap in the caul. Brush with olive oil.

Have ready a well-heated, well-oiled barbecue grill, set about 5 inches above coals of moderate heat. Place the liver on the rack with the seam of the caul set downward. For pink, juicy liver, cook for about 10 minutes on each side, or until the liver feels just firm when you press it gently with your fingers.

Remove the liver to a warm place – such as the cool part of the barbecue or a very low oven – and leave it to rest for 10 to 15 minutes. Transfer the liver to a wooden board, grind over some pepper, then carve into slices. Arrange on a serving platter, garnish with lemon and watercress and serve hot.

# MUSHROOM CAPS
## FILLED WITH CHERVIL BUTTER

When available, fresh ceps may replace mushrooms in this recipe, with excellent results.

Work the butter with a fork and incorporate the chervil, seasoning and lemon juice. Form into balls or pats of a size to fit the mushroom caps. Cover and refrigerate.

   Rapidly rinse and dry the mushrooms, then trim the stems even with their caps, so that they will sit level on the grill. Brush each mushroom liberally with oil, and season.

   Place the mushrooms, stem-side down, on the barbecue grill, over medium-hot coals, and cook for about 10 minutes, turning once halfway through cooking. Transfer the mushrooms to a heated serving dish. Place a piece of butter in each cap, and serve immediately.

### INGREDIENTS

5 oz (1 ¼ sticks) unsalted butter, at room temperature

about 3 tbsp finely chopped fresh chervil or marjoram

salt and freshly ground pepper

1 tsp lemon juice

6 very large mushrooms, about 3 inches in diameter, or 12 medium-size ceps

light olive oil for brushing mushrooms

**Serves 6**

# TURKEY AND SHRIMP BROCHETTES

The brochettes may be served just as they are, or with Saffron Rice (page 74) and Tomato and Sweet Pepper Sauce (page 71).

To make the marinade, crush the garlic to a pulp with a pestle and mortar. Add the lemon juice, paprika, tomato paste and seasoning and mix well. Combine with the cream. Stir in the celery.

   Put all of the ingredients for the brochettes, except for the bay leaves, into a large, shallow dish. Pour over the marinade and mix well. Cover and leave in a cool place or in the refrigerator to marinate for 1 to 2 hours.

   Drain the ingredients, reserving the marinade, and thread them on to six skewers, alternating shrimp, green pepper, turkey and red pepper, and arranging a bay leaf at each end. Baste with a little of the reserved marinade.

   Arrange the brochettes on the barbecue grill set about 6 inches above medium-hot coals. Cook for about 5 minutes on each side, basting regularly with the marinade. Transfer to a heated serving dish and serve.

### INGREDIENTS

FOR THE MARINADE

3 small garlic cloves

3 tbsp lemon juice

½ tsp paprika

2 tsp concentrated tomato paste

salt and freshly ground pepper

¾ cup heavy cream

2 celery stalks, very finely chopped

FOR THE BROCHETTES

1 ½–2 lb boneless turkey breast, cut into equal-sized cubes

24 cooked medium-size shrimp in shell, complete with heads

2 medium-size sweet red peppers, seeded, cut into 1 ¼ in pieces

2 medium-size sweet green peppers, seeded, cut into 1 ¼ in pieces

12 bay leaves

**Serves 6**

# SAFFRON RICE

## INGREDIENTS

2 tbsp unsalted butter

1–2 tbsp olive oil

2 cups long-grain rice

3½ cups water

salt

½ tsp powdered saffron, dissolved in 2 tbsp boiling water

3 cloves

1 cinnamon stick

2 bay leaves

freshly ground pepper

**Serves 6**

In a large saucepan, heat the butter and oil. Stir in the rice and, when the grains are coated, add the water and a little salt. Bring to a light boil, uncovered. Add the saffron and stir once, then add the flavorings of clove, cinnamon and bay. Adjust the heat, with the lid set slightly askew, to maintain a gentle simmer and cook for about 15 minutes or until the liquid is absorbed and the rice tender.

Remove the flavorings. Add pepper to taste. Transfer the rice to a warmed serving dish, fluffing it up slightly with a fork.

# NOISETTES OF LAMB MARINATED IN MINT AND YOGURT

## INGREDIENTS

large bunch of fresh mint, washed and well-dried

2 cups thick plain yogurt

1½ tbsp white wine vinegar

salt and freshly ground pepper

12 noisettes of lamb (boneless loin slices), about 1 in thick and weighing about 2 lb in total

## FOR THE GARNISH

bay leaves

**Serves 6**

In this dish, the yogurt and mint marinade later becomes the accompanying sauce. If you like a lot of sauce, increase the quantities of mint, yogurt and white wine vinegar by half as much again. The yogurt that I most like to use is Greek cow's milk yogurt.

Finely chop the mint leaves using a stainless-steel knife; you should have about 7 tablespoons. In a bowl, mix together the yogurt, vinegar and mint, then add seasoning. Arrange the lamb in a dish in a single layer and coat with the yogurt mixture. Cover and leave to marinate in a cool place for several hours.

Remove the lamb from the marinade. Transfer the marinade to a saucepan ready to heat and serve as an accompanying sauce.

Place the lamb on the oiled barbecue grill, over medium-hot coals, and cook for 5 to 10 minutes on each side. Meanwhile, gently heat through the yogurt marinade; do not let it get too hot or it will separate. Serve the lamb on a bed of Saffron Rice (above) if you like, garnished with a few bay leaves. Offer the sauce separately.

*Noisettes of Lamb with Mint and Yogurt*

# OIL AND PERSILLADE MARINADE

This suits a range of meat and fish brochettes. Use it as an alternative marinade for either the Turkey and Shrimp Brochettes or the Noisettes of Lamb.

Using a pestle and mortar, crush the garlic with a little salt to make a smooth paste. Add the thyme, parsley, lemon zest and a few grindings of black pepper. Combine with the lemon juice, wine and oil.

### INGREDIENTS

| |
| --- |
| *2–3 garlic cloves* |
| *salt* |
| *1 tbsp dried thyme* |
| *3 tbsp finely chopped fresh parsley* |
| *finely grated zest and juice of ½ lemon* |
| *freshly ground pepper* |
| *⅔ cup dry white wine* |
| *6–7 tbsp good quality olive oil* |

# P I N E A P P L E   A N D   O R A N G E
# B R O C H E T T E S
## W I T H   A   S T R A W B E R R Y   C O U L I S

### INGREDIENTS

2 oranges, scrubbed

2 small pineapples

about ⅓ cup sugar

6 tbsp kirsch

1½ lb strawberries

pinch of salt

a little extra sugar for
    caramelizing (optional)

**Serves 8**

The success of these brochettes depends on cutting the fruit in an attractive way. You could also thread slices of banana on to the skewers and, later in the summer, raspberries could replace the strawberries.

Slice the oranges without peeling them, cutting crosswise at ½- to ¾-inch intervals. Cut each slice into four to make fan shapes; transfer to a bowl.

Cut off and discard the leafy tops of the pineapples. Trim each pineapple base to make it level. Slice down the pineapple to remove the skin, then pick out the spiky black 'eyes' with the tip of a small knife. Cut each pineapple into quarters lengthwise. Slice across each quarter – on a plate to catch the juices – to make fan shapes about the same size as those of the oranges. Add the pineapple fans to the bowl.

Sprinkle the oranges and pineapple with the sugar, pour over the kirsch and mix gently but thoroughly so that all the fruit is coated. Cover and leave to macerate in a cool place for 1 to 3 hours.

Meanwhile, mash the strawberries lightly, then purée them by pressing them with a wooden spoon through a nylon strainer set over a bowl. Add a pinch of salt to the purée. Set aside, covered.

Thread the fruit on to skewers, alternating pineapple and orange. Tip the macerating juices into the strawberry purée. Taste and, if you like, add more sugar. Set aside.

Arrange the brochettes on the barbecue grill, set about 4 inches above medium-hot coals, and cook for about 5 to 7 minutes on each side. For a caramelized surface, sprinkle a small amount of sugar over the fruit, but be very careful not to let the sugar fall on to the coals.

To serve, pour a pool of strawberry coulis on to each individual serving plate and put the fruit – removed from its skewer – on top. Alternatively, you can pile all the brochettes on a serving platter and let guests help themselves to brochettes and sauce.

*Opposite: Pineapple and Orange
Brochettes with Strawberry Coulis*

# ORANGES IN THE ASHES

To make strong packages for the fruit, you'll need two layers of foil for each package; so cut out 12 squares of foil.

With a sharp knife, cut away all peel and white pith from the oranges. Slice each orange crosswise and remove any seeds. Then put the slices back together again, with a small pinch of sugar between each slice, to reform the oranges.

Place each orange on a double-layered square of foil. Drizzle over the liqueur. Gather up the foil and twist the edges upward to make a tall topknot handle that will show above the surface of the ashes when the package is buried.

Bury the packages in a 4–inch deep bed of hot ashes and leave to cook for about 15 minutes. Lift out the packages. Remove and discard the outer layer of foil. For serving, guests can either take a package and unwrap the inside layer of foil for themselves, or you can do it, completing the presentation by sliding each orange on to individual plates, and pouring over the juices. Cream is not strictly necessary, but should be on offer for those who want it.

## INGREDIENTS

6 large oranges

2 tbsp sugar

6 tbsp Grand Marnier or
   Cointreau

about 1 ½ cups heavy cream, to
   serve (optional)

**Serves 6**

# A

# *Vegetarian*

## BRUNCH

With this menu I have tried not only to provide recipes for those who are vegetarian in the strictest sense, but also to suggest some for the less zealous demi-vegetarians who include dairy foods in their diet.

The brunch opens with a home-made muesli packed with an interesting selection of dried fruits and nuts, including ready-to-eat dried apricots and roasted hazel-nuts. The mixture can be eaten as it is, simply moistened with milk, smetana or yogurt. But if you want to transform it into something extra special, you can under-score the apricots and hazelnuts with accompaniments of dried Apricot Purée and Hazelnut and Honey Yogurt. When fresh apricots are in season, and destined for the apricot crumble dessert course, replace the dried apricot purée with a raspberry purée.

Both the Sweet Spinach Gâteau with pine nuts and raisins, and the Mushroom and Thyme Pudding-Soufflé, are bound by eggs. The spinach gâteau is best described as a quiche without the pastry. The addition of pine kernels and raisins serves to reinforce the natural sweetness of the spinach. And it is the hint of sweetness, I think, that makes this dish an attractive proposition early in the day.

The Mushroom and Thyme Pudding-Soufflé is very gentle on the digestion, having the comfortable feel of a pudding about it, although it has a lightish texture. Its base is a firm béchamel, lightened with beaten egg white to produce a mixture that is stable enough to be turned out of a decorative ring mold.

The Bean Feast is a delicious dish for everyone to enjoy, and will satisfy the strictest vegan. It combines four types of beans – red kidney, black-eyed, navy, and aduki – with a rich tomato sauce, plus a little celery for added color. If you find aduki beans difficult to obtain, then simply make up their weight with a little more of the other beans. A salad containing sweet peppers goes well

# SPECIAL-BLEND MUESLI, APRICOT PURÉE, HAZELNUT AND HONEY YOGURT

*Special-blend Muesli with
Apricot Purée and
Hazelnut and Honey Yogurt*

*Sweet Spinach Gâteau
or
Mushroom and Thyme Pudding-Soufflé,
Mushroom Purée
or
Bean Feast*

*Selection of Breads, Rolls and Muffins*

*Apricot Crumble with Almonds*

*Coffee or Tea*

with the Bean Feast, as it does with any of these main courses.

The bean dish could be greatly simplified by including only one type of bean – say, the navy bean – and tomatoes, onions and herbs. In fact, there are many extremely simple vegetable dishes that lend themselves to breakfast and brunch. One of them is button mushrooms or eggplant slices, deep fried in herby bread crumbs and served with seasoned *fromage frais* or yogurt; another is tomatoes, stuffed with a duxelle of mushroom and onion.

Yet another – and a great favorite of mine – is sweet potatoes with honey: bake whole sweet potatoes in a medium oven until just cooked without being flabby, then slice fairly thickly and arrange in a lightly buttered shallow dish, in a single layer of overlapping slices. Add slivers of butter and a drizzling of honey on top, and season. Bake at about 350°, or a fraction lower, for about 30 minutes.

Other simple vegetable dishes could be based on raw vegetables: cucumber, tomatoes, celery, carrots, sweet peppers. These could either be served with, or tossed in, a yogurt-based dressing, perhaps enlivened with lemon juice and fresh mint or basil. Such dishes are frequently eaten for breakfast in the Middle East. In India, simple vegetable mixtures, raw or cooked and often spiced, are enclosed in parathas, which are fried flat breads.

The Apricot Crumble is, by contrast, very English. The flavors of both sweet and bitter almonds, the latter coming from the apricot kernels, overlay that of the fresh apricots. However, I must admit that some people refer politely to bitter almond as an 'acquired' taste; if it isn't yours, then simply discard the kernels. Fresh apricots have a relatively short season; if they are not available use nectarines, peaches, plums or apples, or combinations of these.

The crumble topping is a very thin one. Make sure the fruit is level and flat because there is no allowance for crevices that require extra crumble to fill them. I have used white sugar in the topping for two reasons: one, because the texture of the crumble is better with white and, two, because I find the flavor of brown sugar too assertive for delicate fruit. I have also kept sugar to a minimum, not only because I like a little tartness but also to allow for the indulgence of serving a chilled Sauternes, which should be sweeter than the food it accompanies.

# SPECIAL-BLEND MUESLI
## WITH FRUIT PUREE AND HONEY
## YOGURT

Muesli lends itself well to the addition of virtually any kind of fresh fruit. I also like to stir into individual helpings chewy dried fruits, such as pear or peach, that have been first softened in water.

Combine the ingredients in a large bowl. If you are not going to use the mixture immediately, store it in an airtight container. Serve with Apricot Purée and/or the Hazelnut and Honey Yogurt (below).

## APRICOT PUREE

Instead of moisturized, ready-to-eat dried apricots you can use regular dried apricots that have been soaked for several hours.

Simmer the apricots in water to cover, to which you have added the strip of orange peel, for about 20 minutes. When the apricots are tender, drain, rinse under cold water to cool them, and drain again. Discard the orange peel. Purée in a blender or food processor with the orange juice. Alternatively, purée the apricots using a food mill or strainer.

The purée is ready to serve at this stage; but if you prefer a sweeter, thinner purée, add a light sugar syrup. To make the syrup, dissolve the sugar in the water in a saucepan set over low heat. Raise the heat and, without stirring, let the syrup boil rapidly for about 3 minutes. Cool the syrup quickly by standing the base of the pan in iced water. When the syrup is perfectly cold, stir it gradually into the purée.

## HAZELNUT AND HONEY
## YOGURT

It is not essential to roast the hazelnuts for this recipe, but the roasted flavor does make a difference.

Reserve five or six whole hazelnuts for decoration. Put the remainder in a food processor or nut or coffee grinder and grind the nuts to a powder. Add the yogurt and honey to the nuts and blend everything until smooth.

Turn into a small dish. If you like, chill slightly before serving, decorated with the reserved whole hazelnuts.

### INGREDIENTS

2 cups rolled oats

1 cup wheat flakes

1 cup rye or barley flakes, or a mixture of the two

3 heaping tbsp sunflower seeds

⅔ cup raisins, large ones chopped small

3 tbsp golden raisins

¾ cup shelled hazelnuts (filberts), lightly roasted in a moderate oven for about 20 minutes, then skinned and coarsely chopped or halved

¼ cup very coarsely chopped brazil nuts

½ cup chopped ready-to-eat pitted prunes

¾ cup chopped dried apple

1 cup roughly chopped or quartered ready-to-eat dried apricots

**Makes about 1 ½ pounds**

FOR THE PUREE

1 lb ready-to-eat dried apricots

strip of orange peel

juice of 1 orange

FOR THE SYRUP
(OPTIONAL)

½ cup sugar

⅔ cup water

**Serves 8**

FOR THE YOGURT

1 cup shelled hazelnuts (filberts), lightly roasted in a moderate oven for about 20 minutes, then skinned

2 cups plain yogurt

6 tbsp liquid honey

**Serves 4 to 8**

# SWEET SPINACH GATEAU

## INGREDIENTS

2¾ lb fresh bulk spinach, all tough stems removed then washed, or 1¼ lb frozen chopped spinach

salt

6 extra large eggs

2 cups heavy cream

freshly ground pepper

freshly grated nutmeg

⅓ cup pine nuts

2 tbsp raisins

### FOR LINING THE DISH

2 tbsp dry bread crumbs mixed with 1 tbsp finely grated Gruyère

**Serves 8**

You will need up to 8 ounces less spinach if it is young.

Plunge fresh spinach into plenty of boiling salted water, return to the boil and cook for 1 to 2 minutes. Drain, refresh under cold running water, then drain again and squeeze out excess moisture. Chop the spinach coarsely and set it aside. (Cook frozen spinach according to the package instructions, then squeeze it free of moisture.)

Preheat the oven to 350°.

Butter an 11-inch quiche or tart mold and sprinkle it with the bread crumb and cheese mixture. Rotate the dish to coat it evenly; tap out the excess.

In a large bowl, beat together the eggs and cream. Stir in the spinach and season well with salt, pepper and nutmeg. Pour the mixture into the prepared dish. Distribute the pine nuts and raisins evenly throughout the mixture. Bake for 45 to 50 minutes or until lightly set.

Remove the gâteau from the oven and let it stand at room temperature for about 5 minutes before serving.

# MUSHROOM AND THYME PUDDING-SOUFFLE

## INGREDIENTS

6 tbsp unsalted butter

6 tbsp all-purpose flour

1½ cups milk

6 extra large or 7 large eggs, separated

Mushroom purée (opposite page)

### FOR THE MUSHROOMS

1 lb 2 oz button mushrooms

4 tbsp unsalted butter

1 tbsp olive oil

1½ tbsp dried thyme

salt and freshly ground pepper

pinch of quatre épices

**Serves 8**

Rinse the mushrooms rapidly and dry them well on cloths or paper towels. Either slice them finely, or chop them coarsely using a food processor if you wish. In a wide sauté pan set over a low heat, melt the butter with the oil. Add the mushrooms and thyme. Raise the heat and cook for about 4 minutes, shaking the pan to keep its contents moving, until all liquid exuded by the mushrooms has evaporated. Remove from the heat. Season with salt, pepper and *quatre épices*. Set aside.

Prepare a thick white sauce: melt the butter, stir in the flour and cook, continuing to stir, for a few minutes to prevent a floury taste. Raise the heat and whisk in the milk, continuing to whisk until the milk forms a sauce that is smooth and thick, and holds a perfect peak on the whisk. Set aside to cool.

Butter a 4-pint ring mold generously and evenly. Preheat the oven to 350°.

Beat the egg yolks, one at a time, into the cooled sauce. Season lightly. Add the mushrooms, then adjust the seasoning if necessary. Set aside. Have ready some hot water for a *bain-marie*.

Beat the egg whites with a pinch of salt until they just hold a peak. Add one-third of the beaten whites to the mushroom base, stirring quickly with the whisk. Then rapidly and carefully combine this mixture with the remaining whites, lifting and folding the whites with an up-and-over movement, using your hands or a spatula.

Pour the mixture into the mold, then tap it lightly on the work surface to settle. Stand the mold in a suitable container – a roasting pan for instance – to make a *bain-marie*. Transfer it to the oven shelf; pour enough hot water into the *bain-marie* to immerse the mold to two-thirds of its depth.

Cook for about 25 minutes, or until the surface is firm but springy and the sides have shrunk slightly. Remove the mold from the *bain-marie* and cool on a rack for about 5 minutes. Free the sides and turn out the pudding on to a plate. Serve immediately, with Mushroom Purée.

*Sweet Spinach Gâteau with Pine Nuts and Raisins*

# MUSHROOM PUREE

The purée reinforces the basic flavors of the pudding-soufflé.

In a food processor or blender, chop the mushrooms, in batches, to the consistency of medium-sized bread crumbs. Over low heat, melt the butter in a large, heavy frying pan or sauté pan. Add the mushrooms, thyme, lemon juice and seasoning. Cover the pan, raise the heat to medium and cook for 3 to 4 minutes, shaking the pan frequently. Remove the lid and stir briefly over high heat until excess liquid has evaporated and the mixture is soft. Stir in the cream and heat through gently just before serving.

## INGREDIENTS

| |
|---|
| ¾ lb mushrooms, cleaned and, if large, roughly chopped |
| 6 tbsp unsalted butter |
| 1 tsp dried thyme |
| juice of ½ small lemon |
| salt and freshly ground pepper |
| ⅔ cup heavy cream |

**Serves 8**

# BEAN FEAST

## INGREDIENTS

1 cup dried navy or Great
    Northern beans

⅔ cup dried red kidney beans

1 cup dried black-eyed peas

½ cup dried aduki beans

6 cups drained canned tomatoes

2 tbsp unsalted butter

3 tbsp olive oil

2 cups coarsely chopped onions or
    shallots

4 large garlic cloves, finely
    chopped

1 large fresh bouquet garni,
    consisting of thyme, bay,
    parsley, celery leaves and lemon
    peel

1 cup finely sliced celery

2 tsp dried thyme

2 tsp dried oregano

salt and freshly ground pepper

## FOR THE GARNISH

about ¼ cup finely chopped fresh
    parsley

**Serves 8**

Be on your guard with the soaking and cooking times of beans as I have found that timings can vary drastically, depending on the supplier or brand name. And, generally, any type of bean bought loose will be very different from its counterpart in a sealed packet. Another point worth mentioning is that many cookbooks, particularly those written more than 10 years ago, recommend soaking times of up to 24 hours, whereas the average modern bean would have fallen apart well before then.

Pick over the beans, discarding any that are damaged. Soak the beans, according to type, in separate bowls of cold water, for 6 to 8 hours. (While the beans soak, you can, if you like, make the tomato sauce.) Drain the beans and discard the water.

Put the navy or Great Northern beans and the red kidney beans in a large pan and cover with plenty of fresh cold – unsalted – water. Combine the black-eyed peas and the aduki beans in a separate pan of unsalted water. Cover the two pans, set over low heat and bring very slowly to the boil; this will take about 40 minutes. Set the lids slightly askew and simmer rapidly for about 10 to 15 minutes. Drain well and rinse with cold water until the liquid runs clear. Set the beans aside, in their two separate batches.

Purée the tomatoes either by pushing them through a nylon strainer, or by passing them through the finest blade of a food mill, to remove seeds and cores. You should have about 6 cups of tomato purée.

In a large sauté pan with deep sides, heat the butter and oil gently. Sweat the onions for 10 to 15 minutes or until soft. Stir in the garlic and, after a few minutes, add the puréed tomatoes. Stir to amalgamate the ingredients.

Bring the tomato sauce to a simmer. Add the navy or Great Northern beans and red kidney beans, then transfer the mixture to a deep pan or attractive oven-to-table flameproof casserole. Add the bouquet garni. Cover with the lid set partially askew and simmer for 35 minutes.

Add the black-eyed peas and aduki beans, removing the bouquet garni if there is no room in the pan. Add the celery, dried herbs, a little salt, and pepper to taste. Cook for a further 30 to 40 minutes or until the beans are tender enough for your liking. Finally, taste and adjust the seasoning. If you like, keep over very low heat until you are ready to serve, garnished with parsley.

# APRICOT CRUMBLE
## WITH ALMONDS

Cut the apricots in half and pick out the pits. To lend the apricots a bitter-almond flavor, crush the pits to free the kernels and set the kernels aside. Arrange the apricots in a single layer in a wide, heavy-bottomed sauté pan. Sprinkle with the sugar and add enough of the water barely to cover the fruit. Partially cover the pan, set it over low heat, and bring gently to a light boil. Adjust the heat to maintain a gentle simmer and cook until the apricots are soft but still retain their shape – about 15 minutes, depending on the fruit's ripeness.

Transfer the fruit to a lightly buttered shallow baking dish. Moisten with 2 or 3 tablespoons of the poaching liquid; reserve the remainder. Scatter over the reserved kernels supplemented by the coarsely chopped almonds. Set aside.

Preheat the oven to 400°.

To make the topping, sift the flour, salt and sugar into a bowl, then rub or cut in the butter until the mixture resembles large bread crumbs. Spread the mixture over the apricots.

Bake for 20 minutes, then lower the oven temperature to 350° and bake for a further 20 minutes, or until the crumble topping is lightly browned. Scatter the finely chopped almonds over the top 5 minutes before the end of cooking. Serve warm with heavy cream or yogurt blended with a little reserved poaching liquid.

### INGREDIENTS

| |
|---|
| 2 lb fresh apricots |
| 2 tbsp sugar |
| 1 pint water |
| 2–3 tbsp coarsely chopped blanched almonds |

### FOR THE CRUMBLE TOPPING

| |
|---|
| 1 cup self-rising flour |
| pinch of salt |
| ⅓ cup sugar |
| 1 stick unsalted butter, softened |
| ½ tbsp finely chopped blanched almonds |

**Serves 8**

*Bean Feast*

# AN

## Alsace

## CELEBRATION

The excellence of Alsace's hybrid Franco-Germanic cuisine provoked Prosper Montaigne, the author of *Larousse Gastronomique*, to enthuse, 'The Alsace meal is a perfect epicurean symphony.' Even though I could not include all of Alsace's specialities – some, such as foie gras, seemed too expensive, while others, such as wild boar, are too rare – this menu is authentic in that it represents and celebrates distinctive culinary features of the region. The Pain aux Fruits Secs is a version of the centuries-old Birewecke, meaning pear bread. Over the years, the bread gradually became laden with a whole variety of dried fruits – not necessarily including pear at all – and nuts. The dried fruits were tenderized by soaking, usually in a local eau-de-vie or kirsch; and the dough that held the fruits together was flavored with spices such as cinnamon. Other names for this type of bread are Schnitzbrod and Hurzelknopf. Some versions are exceptionally cake-like, employing copious amounts of butter and eggs, while others are totally devoid of such enrichments, so that the background of dough is a plain canvas for the fruits. The version given here is midway between these two extremes.

Pain aux Fruits Secs can be enjoyed on its own as a one-course, informal breakfast. At a more elaborate breakfast it might be served as a final course, with butter and honey. Alternatively, it can be served as an accompaniment to a range of cold smoked meats. The fruit in the bread makes it a particularly good companion for smoked ham, smoked pork and smoked turkey. I also like it with delicate veal sausages.

Bread, in the form of brioche, is also an integral part of Saucisson en Brioche and the Boeuf en Brioche. Laden with butter and eggs, brioche is the richest form of bread. Some consider it more of a cake than a bread, as

# BEEF TENDERLOIN IN BRIOCHE

*Boeuf en Brioche*
(BEEF TENDERLOIN IN BRIOCHE)
*or*
*Saucisson en Brioche*
(POACHING SAUSAGE WRAPPED IN
BRIOCHE)
*or*
*Paupiettes de Veau*
(SMOKED HAM AND KIDNEY WRAPPED
IN VEAL)
*Creamed Mushrooms*
*or*
*Selection of Smoked Meats*

*Tarte aux Pommes*
(APPLE TART, ALSACE STYLE)
*or*
*Pain aux Fruits Secs*
(ALSACE BREAD WITH DRIED FRUITS)

*Digestifs Café*

illustrated by the common translation of Queen Marie-Antoinette's (in)famous remark, when told her people had no bread: 'Qu'ils mangent de la brioche' ('Let them eat cake'). Brioche and beef tenderloin make excellent partners, both having a compatible buttery flavor. And, during cooking, the brioche absorbs some of the savor and juices of both the beef and mushrooms that it envelops.

The sauce calls for wine and good, home-made veal stock. In the absence of such stock, you could use a mild-tasting chicken or vegetable stock. Alternatively, increase the quantity of wine and replace the stock with a little water. Whatever you do, don't use a strong-tasting beef stock or, worse, a beef stock cube – it will be quite the wrong flavor.

This principle about stock also applies to the Paupiettes de Veau, a quick-and-easy assembly of veal cutlets, lined with smoked ham, then wrapped around calf's kidney and tarragon. The smoky flavor of the ham and the assertive taste of the tarragon bring the delicate veal to life.

Smoked ham is only one of a diverse range of smoked meats that are popular in Alsace. A selection of such meats, possibly supplemented with charcuterie inspired by the Alsace region, makes a simple alternative for the main course. True, the Strasbourg sausage is almost impossible to find outside Alsace; but its general make-up of smoked pork and beef is very similar to the frankfurter, which is widely available. Other sausages of the region that you might consider are bockwurst and bratwurst.

Depending on how late the breakfast is served, you might present the sausages with the traditional Alsatian accompaniment of *choucroute* (sauerkraut), a dish that can be too sharp for the delicate palate early in the day. The basic raw sauerkraut takes up to a month to mature, which is a daunting prospect, and impractical for the purposes of this book. But you can often buy decent uncooked sauerkraut at better food stores. Cook it yourself, adding white wine and spices to your liking. Allow two to three hours of cooking for crisp results, or up to five hours if you prefer it tender.

In Alsace, open-faced tarts appear in many guises, their filling frequently bound with a custard of some kind. Generally, it is neighboring Lorraine that specializes in savory versions – nowadays universally referred to as quiches – in which the egg and cream custard holds together such ingredients as ham, cheese, softened onions and mushrooms. Such tarts make excellent fare for a late breakfast, but so many recipes for them already exist that I don't feel justified in giving another. The recipe I give for a sweet version (page 96) can be adapted to a savory one.

Alsace concentrates on sweet tarts that incorporate sumptuous fruits like blueberries, damsons and plums, apricots and cherries. Any of these seasonal fruits might replace the more perennial apples in the recipe provided, which is simple in the extreme. Both the raw pastry shell and raw apples receive their preliminary cooking simultaneously, and the surface of the apples is scored to assist the process. Walnut halves are a welcome, though not essential, addition.

I wouldn't serve a first course with this meal other than perhaps offering a canapé (page 113). But if I omitted the fruit-based dessert, I would open the meal with any of the fresh fruit dishes in this book. You might consider concluding the meal with an Alsatian digestif, such as kirsch, framboise, mirabelle or poire. These eaux-de-vie also make wonderful long drinks. Poire and mirabelle can be mixed with grape juice, ice and club soda or sparkling mineral water. Kirsch and framboise mix well with pineapple juice; add ice and sparkling water if you wish.

# BOEUF EN BRIOCHE
## BEEF TENDERLOIN IN BRIOCHE

## INGREDIENTS

### FOR THE BRIOCHE

3 tbsp sugar

¼ cup lukewarm water

1 tbsp active dry yeast

3⅔ cups bread flour, sifted

1 tsp salt

about ¾ cup lukewarm milk

3 extra large eggs

5 oz (1¼ sticks) unsalted butter, softened and cut into bits

1 extra large egg yolk mixed with 2 tbsp water, for the glaze

### FOR THE BEEF

1 tbsp olive oil

1 tbsp unsalted butter

1 beef tenderloin roast, about 10 in long and weighing just under 3 lb, trimmed of fat and tied to form an even-shaped roll

salt

1½ tbsp dried green peppercorns, crushed

### FOR THE MUSHROOMS

¾ lb equal-sized button mushrooms, cleaned and sliced

2 tbsp unsalted butter

juice of ½ lemon

about 1½ tsp dried thyme

salt and freshly ground pepper

Beef tenderloin, flavored with mushrooms and green peppercorns, is wrapped and cooked in brioche. The beef must be well prepared by the butcher, and tied into a neat shape, with the narrower 'tail' end brought back on itself to even out the overall thickness. A tenderloin roast 10 inches long is the maximum length to fit comfortably into an average-sized sauté pan for the purposes of searing the meat. But you can prepare a longer one if you use a large roasting pan of sufficient weight for searing. The entire preparation is a lengthy one, but it has certain advantages: most of the work, including the sauce-making, can be done the night before; the last stage of cooking is virtually effortless; and the beef's longish resting period leaves the cook free to entertain.

First make the brioche dough: in a small bowl, dissolve the sugar in the water. Add the yeast, then whisk, cover and set aside in a warm place for about 15 minutes or until the mixture foams slightly. Pour the yeast mixture into a large bowl and whisk in one-third of the sifted flour, the salt and the milk. Continue to whisk to make a thick batter. Cover the bowl with plastic wrap and leave to rise in a warm place for about 1 hour or until doubled in volume.

Whisk in the eggs, then whisk in the softened butter a few bits at a time. Stir in the remaining sifted flour a handful at a time to form a loose, sticky dough. Turn out the dough on to a well-floured work surface and knead for 10 to 15 minutes or until smooth and elastic. Return the dough to a clean, dry bowl, cover with plastic wrap and leave to rise in a warm place for 1½ to 2 hours or until tripled in volume.

Meanwhile, prepare the beef. In a heavy sauté pan, heat the oil and butter and lightly brown the beef on all sides – just enough to 'seize' or sear it; this should take about 5 minutes. Remove the beef and reserve the sauté pan, complete with its meaty deposits. When the beef is completely cold, remove the strings, sprinkle it with salt, and coat it with crushed green peppercorns. Set aside in a cool place.

In a frying pan, gently cook the mushrooms in the butter for about 1 minute. Add the lemon juice, thyme and seasoning, then cover the pan and shake it to encourage the juices to flow. Drain the mushrooms in a strainer set over a bowl. Set the mushrooms aside and reserve their juices.

On a floured surface, punch down the brioche dough, then roll it out to a rectangular shape that will envelop the beef. If you like, measure the girth of the meat with string and use it as a guide. Arrange the mushrooms down the middle of the dough, leaving a border clear all around. Lay the beef, with its slightly curved side downward, on the bed of mushrooms and wrap it in the dough, making the seam on the beef's slightly flatter underside. Turn the package over and place it – flatter side down – on a greased baking sheet. Cover with a cloth and set aside for about 45 minutes. Alternatively, keep it in the refrigerator overnight, then leave it at room temperature for about 45 minutes before cooking.

Preheat the oven to 475°. Cook the beef for 10 minutes, then cover the top with foil – or do this sooner if the brioche is browning too quickly. Reduce the heat to 400°. Continue cooking for 25 minutes for exceptionally rare beef and 35 minutes for medium rare.

While the beef cooks, make the sauce: drain off excess fat from the reserved sauté pan and set it over high heat. Add the stock and wine and bring to the boil, scraping the pan to loosen the sediment. Add the Cognac and reserved mushroom juices. Boil again until reduced by about one-third. Strain into a clean pan. If you wish, add the cream and boil again briefly, then add the peppercorns. Adjust seasoning; keep warm until needed.

Five minutes before removing the meat from the oven, take off the foil and brush the brioche with the egg yolk glaze. When the beef is done to your liking, remove it, wrap it in foil and set aside in a warm – but not hot – place, to rest for about 30 minutes. This resting period is essential, particularly if the meat is rare, because during this resting time the blood and juices are reabsorbed back into the meat. Serve sliced, with broiled tomatoes, watercress and the sauce. You could also offer horseradish sauce.

### FOR THE SAUCE

*1 cup Gelatinous Veal Stock (page 32)*

*1 ¼ cups red or white wine*

*⅓ cup Cognac*

*1 cup heavy cream (optional)*

*1 ½ tbsp dried green peppercorns, crushed*

*salt and freshly ground pepper*

### FOR THE GARNISH

*1 small or ½ large tomato per person*

*watercress*

**Serves 12 to 15**

# SAUCISSON EN BRIOCHE
## POACHING SAUSAGE WRAPPED IN BRIOCHE

### INGREDIENTS

*1 large poaching sausage, weighing ½–1 lb, either home-made (page 28 and opposite) or bought*

*⅓ recipe quantity brioche dough (page 90) for every ½ lb of sausage*

*salt*

*little all-purpose flour*

*1 egg yolk mixed with 2 tbsp water, for the glaze*

**Serves 2 to 4, depending on the size of the sausage**

Make the brioche dough. While it is rising, prick the sausage and poach it in lightly salted simmering water. Allow about 25 minutes for a ½-pound sausage and about 40 minutes for a 1-pound sausage. Drain, cool and skin the sausage, then lightly flour it.

On a floured surface, punch down the risen dough and roll it into one or two strips about 2 inches wide. Coil the dough around the sausage, working at a slight angle; press the open ends together. Transfer the sausage package to a greased baking sheet. Cover and leave to rise in a warm place for 1 hour.

Preheat the oven to 425°.

Bake the sausage for 5 minutes, then brush the dough with the egg yolk glaze. Reduce the oven temperature to 400° and continue to bake for about 25 minutes or until the brioche is done; cover with foil if the brioche turns too brown too quickly. Cool the sausage for 10 minutes on a wire rack, then slice and serve. Offer mustard and horseradish sauce as accompaniments.

### POACHING SAUSAGES

Poaching sausages differ slightly from those deemed suitable for frying and broiling. Generally speaking, poaching sausages have a tougher casing – either an ox intestine or a synthetic one – which is unlikely to burst in the poaching water. Another

*Sausage-making*

slight difference is that the texture of the meat in poaching sausages – certainly the commercial varieties – tends to be finer, as witnessed in boudin blanc, frankfurter and bockwurst, for example. But there are no hard and fast rules; and poaching sausages might equally well contain coarse mixtures of meat and even rather chunky pieces of pork fatback. If the sausages have been smoked in their skins, the poaching process rinses away any smoky residues of curing.

To make your own poaching sausages follow the recipe on page 28, introducing the following variations:

Use ox intestine in place of pigs'. Remember that, with an ox intestine, you will not necessarily need a special sausage-making attachment. Ox intestine is large enough to be filled by hand, using a large piping tube or forcing bag fitted with a wide nozzle. For a fine texture, grind the meat once through a medium disc, then once through a fine disc. Alternatively, grind the meat very finely in a food processor. Vary the type of meat to suit your personal taste. Rabbit, game and lamb sausages are among the more uncommon possibilities. A blend of pork and beef is a successful old favorite, as is a mixture of pork and veal. Particularly delicate sausages are made from all veal. Pork fatback, diced, may be included where the meat is exceptionally lean. Other possible additions include spices and herbs, crushed or chopped garlic, truffles and pistachio nuts.

To cook the sausages, prick their skins, then lower them into gently simmering, lightly salted water. Continue to simmer – very gently, to prevent bursting, until done. As a rough guide, allow about 12 minutes for small sausages (frankfurter size); 15 to 20 minutes for something weighing around $\frac{1}{4}$ pound (boudin blanc size); and about 25 minutes for the large French smoked varieties, weighing around $\frac{1}{2}$ pound. An exceptionally large home-made sausage weighing around 1 pound will require about 40 minutes.

# PAUPIETTES DE VEAU
## SMOKED HAM AND KIDNEY WRAPPED IN VEAL

### INGREDIENTS

*1 large calf's kidney, weighing about 1 lb*

*salt and freshly ground pepper*

*6 veal cutlets, weighing 1½–1¾ lb in total, each gently beaten out to 12 × 6 in*

*3–4 tsp chopped fresh tarragon leaves*

*6 slices smoked ham*

*1 tbsp olive oil*

*2 tbsp unsalted butter*

*1½ cups Gelatinous Veal Stock (page 32) or ham stock*

*1 cup Riesling or other dry white wine*

*about ¼ cup heavy cream*

### FOR THE GARNISH

*6 tarragon leaves*

*watercress (optional)*

**Serves 6**

Slices of veal wrapped around smoked ham and calf's kidney are an excellent example of minimal effort for maximum effect. They are delicious. Calf's kidney may have to be ordered in advance from your butcher. In an emergency, it can be replaced with six lambs' kidneys, each one cut in half horizontally, but the flavor will not be as fine. In the absence of fresh tarragon, do not use dried tarragon. Instead, use fresh oregano or marjoram, or a little dried sage or thyme.

Remove the fat and core from the kidney and divide it into six equal-sized pieces. Grind over some pepper and add the tiniest pinch of salt; set aside. Grind pepper over each slice of veal, scatter with tarragon, and lay a slice of ham on top. Place a piece of kidney toward the thin end of each slice of veal and roll it up to form a package; secure with string.

Choose a heavy-based sauté pan – preferably one with straight sides and a lid – that will accommodate the six *paupiettes* comfortably. Heat the oil and butter in the pan, and sauté the *paupiettes* gently on all sides for a few minutes or until very pale golden brown. Drain off any excess fat. Add the stock and wine and bring it to simmering point over medium heat. Closely cover the surface of the *paupiettes* with buttered wax paper, then cover the pan with the lid set askew (or partially cover with foil). Simmer gently for about 30 minutes.

Remove the *paupiettes*. Cut and discard the strings, and keep the *paupiettes* warm in a covered dish. Bring the sauce back to the boil. For a richer sauce, add the cream and boil again. Taste and adjust the seasoning. Arrange the *paupiettes* on a warm serving platter. Garnish each with a tarragon leaf and, if you like, watercress. Serve the sauce separately. Creamed Mushrooms (below) make an excellent accompaniment to this dish.

# CREAMED MUSHROOMS

### INGREDIENTS

*1 lb small button mushrooms*

*½ tbsp olive oil*

*3–4 tbsp unsalted butter*

*salt and freshly ground pepper*

*⅓ cup heavy cream*

*2–3 tbsp finely chopped fresh parsley*

**Serves 6**

Rapidly rinse the mushrooms and dry them well on paper towels. Trim away excess stems and slice the mushrooms thinly. Heat the oil and butter in a large frying pan set over a low to medium heat. When the butter starts to foam, add the mushrooms and cook, stirring, for 1 to 2 minutes. Season lightly. Stir in the cream and continue to cook until the cream reduces and thickens – about 5 minutes. Adjust the seasoning, stir in the parsley and serve.

# SELECTION OF SMOKED MEATS

Allow 4 to 6 ounces of boneless meat per person, and choose a selection that includes smoked pork, smoked venison, smoked turkey, smoked ham and smoked chicken.

Arrange the meats decoratively, preferably on wooden boards. Add a little greenery, such as watercress, parsley, or a chiffonade of lettuce. Position accompaniments, such as a Purée of Sweet Peppers, Extra Creamed Horseradish in Tomato Cases, Crushed Red Currants or Berries in Sour Cream (all on page 105), mustards or Apple Jelly (page 19), and some bread close by.

*Above: Smoked Ham and Kidney Wrapped in Veal (Paupiettes de Veau)*

95

# TARTE AUX POMMES
## APPLE TART, ALSACE STYLE

### INGREDIENTS

#### FOR THE PASTRY

1⅔ cups flour

pinch of salt

2 tbsp sugar

1 stick cold unsalted butter, diced

½ tsp finely grated orange zest

½ tsp finely grated lemon zest

1 extra large egg

2–3 tbsp ice water

#### FOR THE FILLING

3 extra large eggs

6 tbsp sugar

½ tsp ground cinnamon

about ½ cup heavy cream

#### FOR THE FRUIT

2 lb firm, tart apples such as
   Granny Smith

juice of ½ lemon

1–2 tbsp sugar (optional)

few walnut halves (optional)

#### FOR THE GARNISH

½–1 tbsp confectioners' sugar
   (optional)

**Serves 10**

For this apple tart I cut the apples into quarters, then score them to enable the heat to penetrate them evenly. A Gewürztraminer, with its hint of spice and fruit, is a delightful accompaniment if you are serving wine.

First make the pastry: sift the flour, salt and sugar into a large bowl, then rub or cut in the butter until the mixture resembles large crumbs. Add the zest, distributing it evenly. Make a well in the center and drop the egg into it, then mix everything together by drawing in the rubbed-in mixture and adding just enough of the water to form a dough. Cover in plastic wrap and chill for at least 30 minutes.

Lightly grease a 12-inch tart pan. On a lightly floured surface, roll out the pastry dough and use to line the pan. Prick the bottom and sides all over with a fork. Cover and chill while making the filling.

Beat the eggs, sugar and cinnamon together for a few minutes, then stir in the cream. Set aside.

Preheat the oven to 425°.

To prepare the fruit, peel the apples and cut them into quarters (or eighths if the apples are large). As they are prepared, drop them into water acidulated with the lemon juice to prevent them from turning brown. Cut away the core from each quarter and trim the under-side to make a flat surface. On the curved side of each quarter, cut a criss-cross of deep incisions.

Pat the apples dry and arrange them, curved side up, in the pastry case. If the apples are rather tart, sprinkle them with the sugar. Bake for 25 to 30 minutes, checking after 15 minutes and covering the pastry edges with foil if they are browning too quickly.

When the apples are just tender, reduce the oven temperature to 350°. Add the walnuts, if you are using them. Give the filling a stir, then pour it gently into the pastry case. Continue to cook the tart for about 30 minutes, testing with a knife after 25 minutes to see if the filling is set.

Remove the tart from the oven. Leave to stand for 10 minutes or so, then sift a little confectioners' sugar over the surface just before you present it.

*Opposite: Apple Tart, Alsace Style (Tarte aux Pommes) with a Gewurztraminer wine and Alsace Bread*

# PAIN AUX FRUITS SECS
## ALSACE BREAD WITH DRIED FRUITS

### INGREDIENTS

3 tbsp sugar

¼ cup lukewarm water

1 tbsp active dry yeast

5 cups bread flour, sifted

1 tsp salt

⅞ cup lukewarm milk

3 extra large eggs

½ lb (2 sticks) unsalted butter,
softened and cut into bits

finely grated zest of ½ orange

finely grated zest of 1 lemon

1 tsp ground cinnamon

pinch of freshly grated nutmeg

about ¼ cup quartered ready-to-
eat prunes

¾ cup quartered ready-to-eat dried
apricots

½ cup quartered ready-to-eat dried
pears or peaches

⅔ cup raisins

3 tbsp golden raisins

2 tbsp kirsch

⅓ cup shelled hazelnuts, lightly
roasted in a moderate oven for
15–20 minutes, then skinned
and quartered

¼ cup shelled almonds, lightly
roasted in a moderate oven,
then skinned and slivered

1 extra large egg yolk mixed with
2 tbsp water, for the glaze

**Makes 1 large loaf
(3 pounds dough)**

This well-known bread is laden with dried fruit, nuts and spices.

In a small bowl, dissolve the sugar in the water. Add the yeast, then whisk. Cover and set aside in a warm place for about 15 minutes or until the mixture foams slightly.

Turn the yeast mixture into a large bowl and whisk in one-third of the sifted flour, the salt and the milk. Continue to whisk to make a thick batter. Cover the bowl with plastic wrap and leave to rise in a warm place for about 1 hour or until doubled in volume.

Whisk in the eggs, then whisk in the softened butter a few bits at a time. Whisk in orange and lemon zests, the cinnamon and nutmeg, then gradually stir in the remaining sifted flour a handful at a time to form a loose, sticky dough. Turn out the dough on to a well-floured work surface and knead for 10 to 15 minutes or until smooth and elastic. Return the dough to a clean, dry bowl; cover with plastic wrap and leave to rise in a warm place for 1½ to 2 hours or until tripled in volume.

Meanwhile, put the dried fruits in a shallow bowl or dish. (If the fruits are not the moisturized, ready-to-eat type, simmer them first in water for 20 minutes, or until tender.) Drizzle the kirsch over the fruits and toss them. Cover and set aside.

A few minutes before the dough is ready, drain the fruits, spread them out in a single layer and sprinkle them lightly with flour.

Punch down the dough and, on a well-floured surface, gradually knead in the dried fruits and nuts. If necessary, incorporate a little extra flour if the dough is sticky. Shape the dough into a round or any other shape you wish. Transfer it to a greased baking sheet or loaf pan, cover with a cloth and set aside in a warm place to rise for about 1 hour.

Preheat the oven to 400°. Brush the dough with the egg yolk glaze and bake for 15 minutes. Glaze again and bake for a further 15 minutes. Glaze once more and bake for a final 15 minutes or until the bread sounds hollow when rapped on the base. If necessary, cover the surface loosely with foil to prevent over-browning toward the end of cooking.

Remove the bread from the oven and transfer to a wire rack to cool. You can serve the bread as soon as it is cool or, if you prefer, you can cover it in plastic wrap and serve it a day or two later. Offer butter and honey as accompaniments.

*Opposite: Alsace Bread with
Dried Fruits (Pain aux Fruits
Secs) with honey and butter*

# AN

## *Impromptu*

### ARRANGEMENT

This is an ideal menu for a lazy open-house Sunday, with guests coming and going as they please. The food is designed to suit the relaxed mood: it can be assembled at the last moment, and requires no very special planning. Furthermore, the dishes are all good-natured in that they will retain their flavors for late-comers.

With a help-yourself buffet table you can easily offer an imaginative selection of cold smoked poultry, ham and other meats with unusual accompaniments, and savory fruit salads. This menu also includes hot pancakes; the guests can cook their own if you, or they, prefer, using the batter mixture and fillings that you have previously prepared.

I doubt that any store shelf could ever be devoid of their basic ingredients. And their fillings can comprise virtually whatever else you have to hand; my particular suggestions are those which lend themselves to being kept warm in a low oven. The recipe I give for a filling of Tomato and Ham with Oregano is particularly good-natured, and the tomato base can be adapted to include Mozzarella cheese and torn basil leaves. When there is no need to make fillings in advance and keep them warm, you might try duck or chicken livers, briefly sautéed in butter until pink and juicy; or oysters, heated until their edges curl (page 60). On a sweeter note, the pancakes could be filled with pitted black cherries, heated through with a little cinnamon, or with seasonal strawberries, macerated in orange juice and supplemented with whipped cream. Or you could try dried apricots, softened, chopped and combined with almonds for the filling, and a hot purée of the apricots to serve as a sauce for the whole thing.

If you feel energetic enough to make bread cases, then you might also prepare the Breakfast In One, which is a

# BREAKFAST IN ONE

*Selection of Eye-Openers, Pick-Ups and
Punches*

*Compote of Dried Figs and Prunes
in Port*

*Breakfast in One
or
Cold Meat Platter,
served with accompaniments
Pear and Avocado Salad
Endive and Orange Salad
or
Crêpes,
served with a selection of fillings*

*Selection of Breads and Rolls*

*Coffee or Tea*

novel and delicious way of serving traditional eggs and bacon. The golden bread case containing the eggs and bacon is painted with melted butter and crisped in the oven so that it tastes like a superlative version of fried bread. The joy of it is that you can prepare the case and the bacon lining in advance, and have it ready and waiting. Then, when guests arrive, you simply add the raw egg and the Gruyère topping, and return the case to the oven until the egg is cooked.

For this you need a lot of two- to three-day-old bread, which will usually demand some planning. Ideally, plan to make the cases from your own home-made herb dough (recipe on page 11), baking it in rectangular-shaped pans, rather than free-form. If you haven't made or bought bread well in advance, then remember that as a last-minute arrangement you can always dry out fresh loaves – or spare ones from the freezer – in a low oven.

The Compote of Dried Figs and Prunes in Port makes a suitably fruity first course for a breakfast or brunch, without clashing with the fresh fruit in the savory salads that accompany the meat platter. The compote is also based on ingredients that might be found on the store shelf. If you decide not to serve the meat platter and salads, then you could certainly introduce fresh fruit into the first course. The Sunrise Supreme on page 57 and the Citrus Sundae on page 48 would both make suitable alternatives.

# COMPOTE OF DRIED FIGS AND PRUNES IN PORT

The unusual marriage of fresh thyme and figs is inspired by Richard Olney's recipe for Figs with Thyme from his book *Simple French Food*.

Put the sugar, port and red wine in a large saucepan set over low heat. Bring to a gentle simmer, stirring until the sugar has dissolved. Add the figs and the thyme. Partially cover the pan and leave to simmer for 15 minutes. Add the prunes and simmer for a further 15 minutes or until the fruit is tender; timing will depend on the initial dryness of the fruit.

With a slotted spoon, remove the fruit and transfer it to a serving bowl. Remove and discard the thyme. Boil to reduce the syrup over high heat for about 10 minutes, or until its consistency is to your liking.

Leave the syrup to cool – or cool it rapidly by transferring it to a metal bowl set over ice – then taste it and add the lemon juice and, if you wish, honey. Pour the syrup over the fruit.

You can serve the salad immediately or you can serve it after it has marinated for several hours or overnight in a cold place. A few almonds may be scattered over the fruit just before serving. Yogurt, *fromage frais*, cream or *crème fraîche* make pleasant, though not essential, accompaniments.

### INGREDIENTS

| |
|---|
| ⅓ cup light brown sugar |
| scant 1 cup tawny port wine |
| 1¾ cups red wine |
| 18 dried figs, weighing about 10 oz |
| bunch of fresh thyme, wrapped in cheesecloth |
| 18 pitted prunes, weighing about ½ lb |
| 1–2 tsp lemon juice |
| 1–2 tbsp liquid honey (optional) |
| few blanched almonds, slivered (optional) |

**Serves 6 to 8**

*Compote of Dried Figs and Prunes in Port*

# BREAKFAST IN ONE

## INGREDIENTS

2 rectangular loaves of white
bread, 1–2 days old, each loaf
at least 4½ in tall and 8 in
long

2 sticks unsalted butter, melted

about ¾ cup finely grated
Gruyère cheese

2–3 oz pancetta or Canadian
bacon, very thinly sliced

8 extra large eggs

salt and freshly ground pepper

8 tiny scraps of butter

about 2 tsp heavy cream (optional)

**Serves 8**

*Breakfast in One*

Eggs and bacon, with a hint of Gruyère and cream, are here baked in crispy bread cases. The essential point about the bread for the cases is that it should be of a compact texture. I first made this dish in France where the bread is perilously full of holes; and it was the holes that led me to play safe and to include some grated Gruyère in the bottom of the case to prevent the egg from seeping out. The hint of cheese tasted very good.

Slice off the crusts from the loaves, leaving two neat rectangular shapes. Cut each loaf into eight cubes, each cube about 2 inches tall and 3 inches square.

To make the bread cases, stand one of the cubes upright on a board. Working on the uppermost face of the cube, use the tip of a small sharp knife to score an inner rectangle, leaving an outside margin – which will become the wall of the bread case – of about ½ inch. Gradually work the tip of the knife downward to within ½ inch of the cube's base. Avoid cutting into the base. If you find this difficult, mark the knife blade 1½ inches from its tip with a sticky label, and use this marker as a guide. Using your fingers, remove the inner rectangle of bread, scraping the sides and bottom of the case smooth with a spoon. Hollow out the remaining cubes of bread.

Preheat the oven to 375°. Brush the cases, inside and out, with the melted butter, and place them on a baking sheet. Bake for about 15 minutes, or until crisp and pale gold in color. Remove from the oven and put 1 teaspoon of Gruyère in the bottom of each case. Set aside. Reduce the oven temperature to 325°.

Remove any rind and excess fat from the bacon and broil or fry it. Cut or break it into small pieces and distribute it evenly in the bread cases. (If you like, you can set the cases aside at this stage, and finish them later.)

To complete the assemblies, break an egg into each case. Season and add a tiny scrap of butter and, if you like, a small blob of cream to each. Finally, add 1 tablespoon of Gruyère. Bake for about 18 minutes, or until the egg is cooked to your liking. Serve immediately.

# COLD MEAT PLATTER

Allow 4 to 6 ounces of boneless meat per person, and make a selection that includes: poached or smoked chicken; smoked turkey; smoked and unsmoked ham; prosciutto; *bresaola* (Italian cured beef) and pastrami. Arrange the meats decoratively, interspersed with roasted, salted almonds or macadamia nuts and greenery, on a large platter. Spoon a little Purée of Sweet Peppers (below) over the chicken. Add more color with radishes and sliced olives. Place Extra Creamed Horseradish in Tomato Cases near the *bresaola* and pastrami. Arrange a few endive leaves with orange segments in them near the ham.

Surround the platter with dishes of Crushed Red Currants or Berries in Sour Cream (see below) and Apple Jelly with Oregano (page 19). You might also like to offer mustard. Arrange the Endive and Orange Salad and the Pear and Avocado Salad (both on page 106) on either side of the main platter of meat.

## SOME ACCOMPANIMENTS
## FOR COLD MEATS

*Purée of Sweet Peppers*: made by broiling and skinning 4 large sweet red peppers, then chopping the deseeded flesh and blending it to a purée in an electric food processor.

*Extra Creamed Horseradish in Tomato Cases*: halve 4 very large tomatoes. Combine their scooped out, chopped flesh with 5 tablespoons of heavy cream whisked to a peak, and 5 table-spoons of home-made or commercial creamed horseradish. Season and spoon into tomato cases. Top with a sprig of fresh coriander (cilantro).

*Crushed Red Currants or Berries in Sour Cream*: put about a cup of red currants or blueberries or blackberries or cranberries into a heavy pan, with enough water to barely cover. Bring to a light boil, then simmer for 5 to 10 minutes or until soft. Strain away excess water. Cool. Add a little salt. Add a little sugar if liked. Combine with ½ cup of sour cream, or sour cream mixed with heavy cream. Chill until ready for use.

# PEAR AND AVOCADO SALAD

### INGREDIENTS

2 large pears

juice of 2 lemons

2 avocados

2 kiwi fruits

½ cucumber, peeled, seeded,
  thinly sliced, salted and drained

### FOR THE DRESSING

1½ tbsp lemon juice

½ cup freshly squeezed orange
  juice

¼ cup liquid honey

6 tbsp hazelnut (filbert) or walnut
  oil

salt and freshly ground pepper

2 tbsp finely chopped fresh mint
  (optional)

**Serves 8 as an
accompaniment**

An arrangement of sweet pears and avocados in a honey-flavored dressing is finished with cucumber and mint.

Peel, quarter and core the pears. Cut each quarter, lengthwise, into thin slices. To preserve their color, either dip the slices in lemon juice or brush them with the juice. Arrange each sliced quarter section in a fan shape on a plate.
  Peel, halve and pit the avocados. Cut each half lengthwise in half again to make quarters, then cut lengthwise into thin slices. Coat these slices with lemon juice and arrange in fan shapes, alternating with the fans of pear.
  Peel and slice the kiwi fruits and arrange with slices of cucumber in the center or on the sides of the plates.
  Combine the ingredients for the dressing and pour over the salads. Include mint only when it is fresh; on no account use dried. When fresh mint is unavailable, omit it from the dressing and – if you have them – garnish with fresh sage leaves.

# ENDIVE AND ORANGE SALAD

### INGREDIENTS

4 large oranges

salt and freshly ground pepper

5 large heads of Belgian endive,
  trimmed of core and outer leaves

about ½ cup olive oil

juice of ½ lemon

**Serves 8**

Working over a bowl to catch the juice, peel the oranges, removing all the white pith. Extract the segments by cutting on either side of the membrane (page 48). Squeeze the emptied membrane to extract the last of the juice. Strain off about 6 tablespoons of orange juice to use in the dressing. (Use any remaining orange juice for breakfast drinks.) Season the orange segments and set aside.
  Separate the endive leaves and arrange them in a large mixing bowl. Season with a little salt and lots of pepper. Drizzle over about 6 tablespoons of the oil and, with your hands, gently turn the leaves in the oil, ensuring that each leaf is evenly coated. Arrange the leaves, hollow-side up, in a single layer on a large serving dish – or on two smaller ones. Nestle the orange segments in the leaves.
  For the dressing, combine the lemon juice, the reserved orange juice and the remaining oil. Season to taste. Minutes before serving, no sooner, drizzle this dressing over the salad.

# CREPES

Sift the flour and salt into a large mixing bowl. Make a well in the center, add the eggs and mix the two elements by stirring gently with a whisk; start at the center and gradually draw in flour from the sides. Gradually add the milk, stirring rather than beating, until all is smooth. Stir in the oil and Cognac. Strain the batter into a jug and stir in the lemon zest. If you are not ready to use the batter straight away, cover it and set aside in a fairly cool place.

When you wish to make the crêpes, have ready the following: a pad of paper towel dipped into some oil; a spatula; a fork for stirring the batter from time to time; and a seasoned and oiled crêpe pan with a 7-inch base.

Set the pan over medium heat and wait for it to become hot enough to cause a drop of water, flicked from the finger, to sizzle. Pour in just enough batter to cover the bottom of the pan, then tilt it to spread out the batter thinly, finally pouring back any excess batter into the jug. This pouring action will cause a dribble of batter to form up the side of the pan; cut it away. Cook the crêpe for 20 to 30 seconds, at which point the edges should start to curl. Turn the crêpe over and cook the other side for about 15 seconds or until golden. Slide the crêpe out of the pan. Cook the remaining crêpes in the same way, re-oiling the pan whenever it looks dry.

If you intend to serve the crêpes immediately, stack them directly on top of each other, on a warm plate. If, however, you want to make them in advance you can keep them warm by stacking them, wrapping them in foil and placing them in a low oven. If you plan to reheat the crêpes at a later stage, cool each one on a wire rack or on a piece of paper towel; don't stack or overlap them. When they are cold, layer them with plastic wrap, then cover them in plastic wrap or foil and keep for several days in the refrigerator. You may, of course, prefer to cook the crêpes to order when guests arrive, or let guests cook their own.

Fill the crêpes, roll or fold them and serve hot.

## INGREDIENTS

| |
|---|
| 1 ¼ cups all-purpose flour |
| pinch of salt |
| 3 extra large eggs |
| scant 2 cups milk |
| 1 tbsp light oil |
| 1–2 tbsp Cognac |
| finely grated zest of ½ lemon |

**Makes 16 to 18**

# CREPE FILLINGS

4 large ripe tomatoes, weighing
  about 1 ½ lb in total

2 tbsp unsalted butter

½ tsp dried oregano

salt and freshly ground pepper

2 oz lean cooked ham, very thinly
  sliced, chopped small

**Fills 4 crêpes**

### INGREDIENTS

¾ lb small button mushrooms

3 tbsp unsalted butter

3 tbsp fresh chervil or parsley
  leaves snipped into small pieces

3 tbsp heavy cream

salt and freshly ground pepper

squeeze of lemon juice

**Fills 4 crêpes**

### INGREDIENTS

5 oz (about 1 cup) pitted prunes

3 pinches of ground cinnamon

½ cup fresh creamy white cheese,
  such as pot cheese, or thick
  plain yogurt

**Fills 4 crêpes**

## TOMATO AND HAM WITH OREGANO

This simple, fresh-tasting filling can either be made in advance
or left to the last moment.

Loosen the skins of the tomatoes by plunging them briefly into
hot water and then into cold. Peel and core them, cut in half
and remove the seeds. Chop the flesh coarsely. Melt the butter
in a frying pan set over a low heat. Add the tomatoes, then raise
the heat. Add the oregano, rubbing it through your fingers to
release its flavor. Cook, stirring, for 2 to 3 minutes. Season to
taste.
  Add the ham and continue to cook, stirring all the time, until
excess liquid evaporates and the mixture holds its shape – about
3 minutes. Transfer the filling to a warm dish, cover and keep
warm until you are ready to use it.

## MUSHROOMS WITH CHERVIL AND CREAM

Fresh chervil makes this very special. In its absence, do not be
tempted to use dried chervil – use fresh or dried thyme, or fresh
parsley.

Rapidly rinse the mushrooms and dry them well on paper
towels. Trim away excess stems and slice the mushrooms very
thinly. Melt the butter in a frying pan over low to medium
heat. When the butter starts to foam, add the mushrooms and
stir continuously for 1 to 2 minutes. Stir in the chervil and the
cream. Taste and season lightly, adding the lemon juice.
Continue to cook until the cream reduces and thickens – about
5 minutes. Adjust the seasoning and transfer to a warm dish.
Cover the mixture and keep warm until you are ready to use it.

## PRUNES WITH CINNAMON AND FROMAGE BLANC

Simmer the prunes in water to cover until tender – generally
about 20 minutes depending on how dried they were to start
with. Drain well, then chop and sprinkle with the cinnamon.
Set aside until you are ready to fill the crêpes.
  Spread each crêpe with 2 tablespoons of the cheese or
yogurt, leaving a ½-inch border. Add the prunes and roll the
crêpes in the normal way. If you like, reheat the crêpes, in a
covered dish, in a low oven.

## MARMELADE OF APPLES, RAISINS AND ORANGE

Pick over the raisins and remove any stalks. Wash and dry them, then chop small. Peel, quarter and core the apples, dropping them immediately into water containing the lemon juice.

Thickly butter a heavy pan wide enough to contain the apples in a shallow layer. Dry the apples and slice them very thinly. Arrange the apples in the pan in a couple of layers, sprinkling each layer with sugar, orange zest and juice. Press a large circle of well-buttered foil or wax paper on to the apples.

Cook gently for about 5 minutes, or until the apples become translucent; timing will depend on the ripeness and quality of the fruit.

Remove the foil or paper, add the raisins and cook uncovered for a further few minutes or until all excess liquid has evaporated. Transfer the *marmelade* to a warm dish, cover and keep warm until you are ready to use it.

### INGREDIENTS

| |
|---|
| *3 tbsp raisins* |
| *¾ lb firm-textured apples such as Granny Smith* |
| *juice of ½ lemon* |
| *1 tbsp unsalted butter, softened* |
| *1 tbsp sugar* |
| *juice and grated zest of ½ orange* |

**Fills 4 crêpes**

*Crêpes, with a selection of fillings*

# A

## Birthday

BENDER

I have long thought that evening birthday parties are cruel and untimely, in that they withhold the pleasures of seeing friends and opening gifts until the day is virtually over. Consequently, I get celebrations under way as early as possible.

Apart from establishing a cheerful mood at the outset, a breakfast celebration has other advantages: the menu can be simpler than that for a full-blown luncheon or dinner party, thus involving little washing-up; you also have the afternoon free to enjoy yourself, and can still have the evening earmarked for a memorable outing if you choose.

Although the menu is designed with a fairly large-scale birthday party in mind, it could equally well be indulged in by just one person. The main point is that the food is designed to complement Champagne. As an alternative, you could serve a dry white Loire wine, such as a Sancerre, with the first and main course. Or you might try a medium-dry Gewürztraminer from Alsace. With the birthday cake, a Sauternes or Montbazillac would be a good alternative to Champagne. Another point worth mentioning is that all the food can be eaten with a fork alone and easily consumed standing up; so you needn't worry if there are more guests than chairs.

For the main course I have included a pretty Salmon and Spinach Roulade and two types of kedgeree – a rich salmon version and a simpler, more traditional one using smoked haddock. Kedgeree evolved from *khichri*, a spicy mixture of rice and lentils served with fish and meat; the Victorians brought the rice and fish version to the English breakfast table. My versions evoke the Indian origins of the dish. Both are flavored with turmeric and cayenne. The red and green sweet peppers would not have been included, but they are a very good addition.

The finale to this menu is the large four-tiered cake, a

# KIRSCH-SOAKED FANTASY BIRTHDAY CAKE

*Champagne or a selection of cocktails*

*Caviar and Sour Cream Canapés*
*Parma Ham and Fig Croûtes*

*Salmon and Spinach Roulade*
*or*
*Salmon Kedgeree*
*or*
*Traditional Kedgeree of Smoked*
*Finnan Haddie*

*Kirsch-Soaked Fantasy Birthday Cake*
*or*
*Simple Almond Cake*

*Coffee*

wonderful kirsch-soaked fantasy that is an inspiring choice for any celebration – it does not have to be a birthday. I have made it with a génoise sponge, which can be prepared in advance and frozen. If you do not feel like such an extravaganza or the effort involved, then consider making the Simple Almond Cake, which takes no time at all and marries very well with Champagne and Sauternes alike.

A late-morning bender of this kind does presuppose that your guests are free during what amounts to 'normal' working hours. If your friends are not all night-club owners or late-night bus drivers and are guilt-stricken about taking time off work, but you still want to celebrate this way, you will simply have to abandon your real birthday for an 'official' one at a weekend.

# CAVIAR AND SOUR CREAM CANAPES

Carefully separate the slices of pumpernickel and cut each slice in half one way, and into three the other, to give six more or less equal 1½-inch squares. Arrange the squares on a flat serving dish or plate.

Spoon just over ½ teaspoon of sour cream on to the center of each piece of pumpernickel and spread out slightly into a round. Top each with a little caviar, leaving a white surround.

Garnish with small, neat wedges of lemon and serve immediately.

## INGREDIENTS

3 slices dark pumpernickel bread

½ cup sour cream

1½ oz (about 2½ tbsp) caviar

### FOR THE GARNISH

wedges of lemon

**Makes 18**

# PARMA HAM AND FIG CROUTES

Fresh figs and prosciutto are a classic combination, the sweetness of the figs offsetting the slight saltiness of the ham. When fresh figs are out of season, you can replace them with dried figs, reconstituted in a mixture of wine and water or weak tea, with a little honey added.

Butter the slices of bread very thinly, then cut each slice in half one way, and into three the other, to give six more or less equal 1½-inch squares.

Trim excess fat from the ham and cut each slice in half lengthwise to make strips about 1½-inch wide – the same width as the bread. Place the ham on the bread, preferably arranged in little pleats. To do this, drape the end of the strip of ham on to a piece of bread, then fold the ham into a three-layered pleat; cut away excess ham with scissors, and proceed to the next piece of bread, and so on.

Trim the stalks from the figs and cut each fig into four slices. Put a slice of fig on each croûte and serve immediately.

## INGREDIENTS

4 slices light rye or pumpernickel bread

small amount of softened unsalted butter for spreading

about ¼ lb Parma ham or prosciutto, very thinly sliced

5 fresh ripe figs

**Makes about 20**

# SALMON AND SPINACH ROULADE

## INGREDIENTS

1¼ lb fresh bulk spinach, or 1 lb frozen chopped spinach

9 oz (1 heaping cup) ricotta cheese, sieved

⅔ cup heavy cream or crème fraîche

salt and freshly ground pepper

freshly grated nutmeg

4 tbsp unsalted butter

6 tbsp all-purpose flour

1 cup milk, scalded

5 extra large eggs, separated

5 oz smoked salmon, cut into strips

### FOR THE GRATIN FINISH

a little melted butter

about 1 tbsp fine dry white bread crumbs

### FOR THE GARNISH

about 2 tbsp finely chopped fresh parsley

small wedges of lemon

greenery, such as watercress or a chiffonade of lettuce

**Serves 12**

This is a very pretty party dish. Serve it partially sliced to reveal the swirls of pink, green and white. Its arresting appearance belies the simplicity of its preparation and the economy of its ingredients: a little smoked salmon goes a long way in this roulade.

Oil a jelly roll pan 12 × 9 inches, then line the pan with nonstick baking parchment paper. If you do not have a suitable pan, you can make an improvised paper container for the roulade (see below).

Pick over the fresh spinach, discarding all tough stems and any poor-quality leaves; you should be left with about 14 ounces. Wash the spinach thoroughly, then immerse it in plenty of boiling salted water and boil rapidly for 1 to 2 minutes. Drain and refresh under cold water. Drain again, squeeze dry and chop finely. If using frozen spinach, let it thaw, then drain thoroughly. Set aside.

Beat the ricotta smooth. In a separate bowl, whip the cream to soft peaks, then blend it into the ricotta. Stir in just under half of the spinach. Season well, adding a little nutmeg. Set this filling aside.

Melt the butter in a heavy saucepan set over medium heat. Stir in the flour and cook for 1 to 2 minutes, stirring to prevent browning. Whisk in the warm milk and continue to whisk briskly to make a smooth sauce. Cook over extremely low heat for about 5 minutes, stirring occasionally, then set aside to cool slightly.

Preheat the oven to 375°. Beat the egg yolks into the cooled sauce base one at a time, then beat in the remaining spinach. Taste and adjust seasoning. Beat the egg whites to firm – but not dry – peaks. Stir about one-third of the whites into the roulade mixture, then fold in the remainder, taking care not to overmix.

Pour the roulade mixture into the pan and smooth it over. Bake for 15 minutes or until firm to the touch. Remove from the oven and cover with a dish towel that is considerably larger than the pan. Reverse the roulade base on to the towel and lift away the pan. When the roulade base has cooled slightly, remove the paper lining and, if necessary, trim the edges of the roulade base to neaten them.

Spread the ricotta and spinach filling over the roulade base, leaving a 1-inch margin on the long sides of the rectangle. Arrange the strips of salmon running parallel with the longer sides. Roll up the roulade from a long side, fairly tightly, using the towel to help. Place the roll seam-side downward on a serving dish.

The roulade may be eaten immediately, or a little later when it is just cold. For an attractive presentation, partially slice it to reveal the pretty interior. Put a long ribbon of chopped parsley on top. Surround with lemon wedges and some greenery such as bouquets of watercress or a *chiffonade* of lettuce.

To serve the roulade hot, and give its surface a light, golden crust, brush it with melted butter, sprinkle with fine bread crumbs and return to a preheated 350° oven to bake for 5 to 10 minutes or until the top has colored to your liking.

## MAKING A PAPER CONTAINER
## FOR THE ROULADE

If you do not have a jelly roll pan, you can make a roulade in a paper container. Have ready a flat baking sheet about 12 × 9 inches. Cut a rectangle of nonstick baking parchment paper ¾ inch wider than the baking sheet on all sides, so that you have a margin that will ultimately form the sides of the container. Fold over this margin so that it corresponds to the size of the sheet, pressing with your fingers to make a distinct crease. To create the stand-up sides, cut along one of the creases at each corner – cutting only as far as the edge of the sheet – then fold the longer piece of paper on to the shorter one, and secure with paper clips.

*Salmon and Spinach Roulade*

# SALMON KEDGEREE

## INGREDIENTS

2½ lb fresh salmon on the bone, preferably divided into 4 equal steaks

4 bouquets of parsley

4 pinches of salt

16 black peppercorns

½ cup dry white wine, fish stock or water

2 cups long-grain rice

1 large sweet red pepper, cored, seeded and cut into small pieces

1 large sweet green pepper, cored, seeded and cut into small pieces

4–5 hard-cooked eggs, quartered

1 stick unsalted butter

about 2 tsp turmeric

small pinch of cayenne

salt and freshly ground pepper

about 6 tbsp heavy cream

¼ cup finely chopped fresh parsley

lemon juice

### FOR THE GARNISH

about 2 tbsp finely chopped fresh parsley

wedges of lemon

**Serves 10 to 12**

A convenient way of buying and handling the salmon is to purchase four 1 ½-inch thick steaks, each about 11 ounces. But you may prefer to buy two larger steaks or one whole piece of salmon. And certainly if your fishmonger has a tail-end – which is often cheaper – then it would make sense to buy it.

Preheat the oven to 300°.

Prepare a lightly buttered foil parcel for each piece of salmon. Add a bouquet of parsley, pinch of salt, 4 peppercorns and 2 tablespoons wine to each, and close them securely. Bake for about 20 minutes or until barely cooked.

When the fish is cool enough to handle, remove it from the bone and flake it into large pieces, discarding any skin. Set the fish aside. Discard the foil and flavorings.

Cook the rice in lightly salted boiling water to a slightly underdone stage, then drain it. If you are not planning to assemble the kedgeree immediately, rinse the rice under cold water to arrest its cooking, then drain it again; set it aside.

To finish the dish, use two large, heavy sauté pans and divide the ingredients equally between them. First, melt the butter and, when just foaming, put in the rice, about half the turmeric, the cayenne and the sweet peppers. Stir for 1 to 2 minutes, then add the fish. Ensure that the kedgeree is well-seasoned, and add more turmeric accordingly. Heat everything through, shaking the pans frequently and stirring occasionally to prevent sticking. Add the hard-cooked eggs and gradually incorporate the cream. When piping hot, stir in the chopped parsley and lemon juice. Pile on to a warm serving dish and garnish with parsley and wedges of lemon.

*Salmon Kedgeree*

# TRADITIONAL KEDGEREE OF SMOKED FINNAN HADDIE

Soak the smoked fish briefly in cold water, or just rinse it to remove any excess salt. Drain the fish and place it in a wide pan. Add the flavorings and pour over enough cold water barely to cover the fish. Partially cover the pan and bring slowly to a light boil, then simmer for several minutes or until the fish is barely cooked. Remove the fish with a slotted spoon; discard the cooking liquid and flavorings. When the fish is cool enough to handle, remove the bones and skin and flake the flesh into as large pieces as is possible. Set aside.

Cook the rice in lightly salted boiling water to a slightly underdone stage, then drain it. If you are not planning to assemble the kedgeree immediately, rinse the rice under cold water to arrest its cooking, then drain it again. Set it aside.

To finish the dish, use two large, heavy sauté pans and divide the ingredients equally between them. First, melt the butter and, when just foaming, put in the rice, about half the turmeric, the cayenne and the sweet peppers. Stir for 1 to 2 minutes, then add the fish. Ensure that the kedgeree is well-seasoned, and add more turmeric accordingly. Heat everything through, shaking the pans frequently and stirring occasionally to prevent sticking. Add the whites of the hard-cooked eggs, then gradually incorporate the cream. When all is piping hot, stir in the parsley. Remove from the heat. For a richer, stickier texture, remove from the heat and stir in the beaten egg.

Pipe the kedgeree on to a warm serving dish. Rub the yolks of the hard-cooked eggs through a wire strainer over the surface of the kedgeree and garnish with parsley and wedges of lemon.

## INGREDIENTS

4 finnan haddie or other smoked, firm-fleshed fish, weighing about 3½ lb in total on the bone, and about 2 lb off the bone

flavorings: parsley stalks, peppercorns, lemon peel and bay leaf

2 cups long-grain rice

1 large sweet red pepper, cored, seeded and cut into small pieces

1 large sweet green pepper, cored, seeded and cut into small pieces

4–5 hard-cooked eggs, yolks separated and the whites finely chopped

1 stick unsalted butter

about 2 tsp turmeric

small pinch of cayenne

salt and freshly ground pepper

about 6 tbsp heavy cream

¼ cup finely chopped fresh parsley

1–2 eggs, beaten (optional)

### FOR THE GARNISH

about 2 tbsp finely chopped fresh parsley

wedges of lemon

**Serves about 10**

# KIRSCH-SOAKED FANTASY
# BIRTHDAY CAKE

## INGREDIENTS

### FOR THE SPONGE

8 extra large eggs

1 cup superfine sugar

1¼ cups + 2 tbsp all-purpose
flour

6 tbsp unsalted butter, melted

### FOR THE SYRUP

1 cup sugar

1¼ cups water

½ cup kirsch

### FOR THE BUTTER CREAM

8 extra large egg yolks

1 cup sugar

⅞ cup water

1 lb 2 oz (4½ sticks) unsalted
butter, softened

¼ cup kirsch

1 cup shelled hazelnuts (filberts),
roasted for 20 minutes or so in a
moderate oven, skinned and
finely chopped

### FOR THE GLAZE

about ½ cup good quality apricot
preserves

juice of ½ lemon

6 tbsp water

### FOR THE DECORATION

about 1 cup shelled hazelnuts,
roasted, skinned and finely
chopped

about 7 shelled hazelnuts
(filberts), roasted and skinned

I once replaced the butter cream and hazelnut filling of this airy génoise sponge with whipped cream and raspberries. It was just as good.

First prepare two 9-inch diameter cake pans: brush with melted butter, then line the bottoms with nonstick baking parchment paper and brush the paper with a little more melted butter. Lightly coat with flour, rolling the pans around and tipping out the excess flour. Set aside. Preheat the oven to 350°.

To make the sponge, in a large bowl lightly whisk together the eggs and sugar. When the mixture looks pale and creamy, set the bowl over a pan of simmering water placed over low heat. Continue to whisk the mixture with a hand-held electric beater for about 10 minutes.

Remove the pan from the heat with the bowl on top and continue to whisk until the mixture falls from the beaters in a thick ribbon – about 10 minutes longer. Fold in the sifted flour, adding it alternately with the melted butter in four stages. Divide the mixture between the prepared pans and bake for about 30 minutes or until the sponges are firm to the touch at the center and show signs of shrinkage around the edges.

Remove the pans from the oven and place them on a wire rack to cool. After about 5 minutes, unmold the sponges on to the rack; peel away the lining paper and leave to cool completely.

For the syrup, put the sugar and water into a heavy-based saucepan. Stir over gentle heat until the sugar dissolves, then raise the heat and bring the syrup to the boil without stirring. Boil for 2 minutes. Remove from the heat and set the base of the pan in iced water to cool the syrup rapidly. When the syrup is cool, stir in the kirsch. Set aside.

While the syrup is cooling, make the butter cream: beat the egg yolks until pale in a large bowl; set aside. Combine the sugar and water in a heavy saucepan and stir over low heat until the sugar dissolves. Raise the heat, stop stirring and boil the syrup to a short-thread stage – 215° on a sugar thermometer. To test without a thermometer, cool a little syrup on a spoon, then pull it between finger and thumb; it should form a small thread. Remove the syrup from the heat and pour it slowly into the egg yolks, whisking vigorously all the time. Continue to whisk until the mixture cools to a thick, mousse-like texture.

Beat the butter until it is smooth and pale. Gradually whisk in the egg yolk mousse to form a smooth, glossy butter cream. Gradually whisk in the kirsch.

For the filling, transfer just under half the butter cream to a separate bowl and stir in the finely chopped hazelnuts; set aside. Keep the remaining, nut-free butter cream for coating and decorating the cake.

For the glaze, simmer the apricot preserve, lemon juice and water in a saucepan for a few minutes or until the preserve melts. Press through a nylon strainer, then boil for about 5 minutes or until the glaze just drops from the spoon. Set aside.

With a long, serrated knife, slice each sponge in half horizontally. Spoon the syrup gently and evenly over the four layers. If you like, leave the soaked sponge for several hours, to develop the flavor. Carefully transfer one of the layers – to be the bottom layer – to a cakeboard or a serving platter with a flat base.

Spread the top of all the layers with the glaze. Spread only three of the layers – the bottom layer and two other layers – with the hazelnut butter cream filling, leaving the fourth or top layer plain. Stack the three filled layers on top of each other, then place the fourth layer on top.

Coat the top and sides of the assembled cake with nut-free butter cream. If you like, draw the top of the spatula to and fro across the top of the cake to make patterns. Decorate the cake with the remaining butter cream and finely chopped hazelnuts. Scalloped patterns of chopped hazelnuts look pretty, with piped rosettes of butter cream topped with a whole hazelnut. You can also use finely chopped hazelnuts to decorate the sides of the cake, either with scallops or vertical stripes. Candles complete the birthday cake.

*Simple Almond Cake*

# SIMPLE ALMOND CAKE

Preheat the oven to 350°.

Prepare a 9-inch cake pan: brush with melted butter then line the bottom with nonstick baking parchment paper and brush the paper with a little more melted butter. Lightly coat with flour, rolling the pan around and tipping out the excess flour. Set aside.

In a large bowl, beat the butter until smooth, then gradually beat in the sugar until light and fluffy. Beat in the eggs one at a time, then gradually beat in the almonds. When the mixture is well amalgamated, fold in the flour and stir in the almond flavoring.

Transfer the mixture to the prepared pan and tap the pan on the work surface to ensure even distribution. Bake for about 35 minutes or until the cake is firm to the touch in the middle. Turn out on to a wire rack and leave to cool.

Dredge the top of the cake with the sifted confectioners' sugar. Or, if you like, you can sift the sugar over ¾-inch wide strips of cardboard, arranged in stripes or diamonds on the top of the cake, to give an attractive appearance when the strips are removed.

## INGREDIENTS

1 ½ sticks unsalted butter, softened

1 cup superfine sugar

4 extra large eggs

1 ⅔ cups ground almonds

½ cup all-purpose flour, sifted

¼ tsp almond extract

## FOR THE DECORATION

1–2 tbsp confectioners' sugar

# A Romantic

## BREAKFAST FOR TWO

I am convinced that the spark of romance is born in the head. Nevertheless, it can be kindled in a number of different ways.

Certain types of food have an association with love and romance, largely based on Greek and Roman mythology. The ancients placed the roe of sturgeon high in their recommended list of food with provocative powers. More recently, Brillat-Savarin, the French gastronome, spread the idea that 'caviar rouses the instinct of reproduction in either sex.' I find it romantic because, like romance itself, it is rare. Like love, it is costly.

A dish that combines caviar and eggs, another ancient symbol of fertility, seemed an ideal main course for a romantic breakfast. I have given two options. One of them encloses scrambled eggs in slices of smoked salmon. This is an altogether more filling dish than Oeufs à l'Amour, a daring-looking dish of scrambled egg and caviar served in eggshells.

Caviar and romance have a natural affinity with Champagne for me: a fountain of frolicking bubbles that embroiders the imagination and brings forth a sparkle of one's own. But it should be drunk sparingly. We all know the adage about strong waters defeating their own end.

For this menu I suggest exotic fruits, including passion fruit whose tantalizing scent puts romance in the air. To finish, a heart-shaped Coeur à la Crème makes a positive expression of romantic intention.

Make sure there are flowers on the table or tray. Roses, freesias, orchids and spring flowers in general are all winners. Avoid lilies.

Champagne

Oeufs à l'Amour
or
Smoked Salmon Packages

Passion Fruit Salad

Coeurs à la Crème

Coffee or Tea

# OEUFS A L'AMOUR

## INGREDIENTS

2 extra large, fresh eggs

2 tbsp unsalted butter

salt and freshly ground pepper

2 small blobs of heavy cream,
   crème fraîche or sour cream

1 tsp caviar

### FOR THE GARNISH

small pieces of toast, cut into heart
   shapes

**Serves 2**

Gently scrambled eggs are lifted to new heights in this dish –
returned to their shells with caviar.

Using a sharp knife, take the top off each egg, working over
a plate to catch the white as it runs out. Empty the eggs into a
bowl. Wash the shells – bottoms and lids – carefully in warm
water. Set them aside on paper towels to dry. If necessary, trim
the edges of the shells with scissors to neaten them; keep the
shells for presentation.

With a fork, lightly beat the eggs. Scramble the eggs with
the butter. I cook them very slowly in a buttered *bain-marie*,
with the butter cut into tiny cubes, and some salt and pepper
added; and I stir more or less continuously with a wooden
spoon, until the mixture is very soft and creamy.

Fill the two bottom shells with the scrambled egg mixture.
Add a tiny blob of cream to each, then top with caviar. Finally,
put on the lids, so as to resemble little hats. Garnish with small
pieces of toast, cut into hearts.

*Oeufs à l'Amour*

# SMOKED SALMON
# PACKAGES

When you buy the smoked salmon, make sure that it is cut off in four long strips that include the middle section – the widest part of the fish. What you want to avoid is having lots of narrow tail-end slices, with which you will be unable to form neat packages.

To make the two packages, you will need four strips of smoked salmon each about 12 inches long and about 3½ inches wide in the middle. Lay a strip of salmon on each serving plate, then lay another strip across it to form a cross; set aside.

With a fork, lightly beat the eggs and season them. Scramble the eggs to your liking with the butter. An excellent method is to scramble them very slowly in a *bain-marie* (see page 16).

Pile the scrambled eggs in the center of the smoked salmon crosses. Bring over the sides of each cross to make a package and, if you like, trim off any overlap with scissors. Top each package with a teaspoon of caviar, arranged, if you like, in a star shape. Garnish with wedges of lemon, bouquets of parsley and heart-shaped pieces of toast.

## INGREDIENTS

| |
|---|
| 4 long strips thinly sliced smoked salmon, weighing about ½ lb in total |
| 4 large eggs |
| salt and freshly ground pepper |
| 3 tbsp unsalted butter, diced |

### FOR THE GARNISH

| |
|---|
| 2 scant tsp caviar |
| 4 small wedges of lemon |
| 2 tiny bouquets of parsley |
| 4 small pieces of toast, cut into heart shapes |

**Serves 2**

*Smoked Salmon Packages*

# PASSION FRUIT SALAD

## INGREDIENTS

¼ cup sugar

¾ cup water

1 small ripe mango (optional)

2 small, firm kiwi fruits

6 passion fruits

6 kumquats

pinch of salt

juice of ½ lemon

**Serves 2 to 4**

This mixture of tropical fruits is delicious and refreshing on its own; it needs no accompaniment.

Put the sugar and water into a heavy saucepan. Stir over gentle heat until the sugar has dissolved, then raise the heat and bring the syrup to the boil without stirring. Boil the syrup hard for 2 to 3 minutes, then remove from the heat and cool the syrup quickly by setting the base of the pan in iced water.

While the syrup cools, prepare the fruit: if using the mango, peel it and cut through the fruit to remove the pit. Discard the pit and cut the fruit into slices lengthwise. Set aside in a large bowl. Peel the kiwi fruits with a small, sharp knife, and slice into rounds or fan shapes. Add to the bowl. Cut the passion fruits in half and, with a small sharp spoon, scoop out the contents of their shells directly on to the fruit in the bowl. Halve the kumquats and add them.

Pour the cold syrup over the fruit and add the tiniest pinch of salt and the lemon juice. Mix everything together very gently so not to break up the fruit. Serve at room temperature – chilling impairs the flavor and aroma of the fruits – preferably in glass dishes.

### TO PEEL A RIPE MANGO

Score the fruit lengthwise in several places to make four or more sections. Spear the base of the fruit on to a fork. Holding the fork, use a knife to peel back the skin, which will come away according to the scored sections. If you are confronted with a barely ripe mango, you may have to use a potato peeler and a serrated knife.

# COEURS A LA CREME

## INGREDIENTS

¾ cup fresh creamy white cheese
such as pot cheese

⅓ cup crème fraîche or heavy
cream

Coeurs à la Crème molds, made of porcelain and shaped like a heart, have holes in the base that allow excess liquid to drain. In the absence of these molds, you can improvise by cutting down yogurt cartons that are about 3¾ inches in diameter to a height of about 1½ inches, then making small holes in the bottom using scissors. If you use yogurt cartons, double the quantities of cheese and cream.

Wet two small squares of cheesecloth and thoroughly wring out so that they are just damp. Line two Coeurs à la Crème molds with a single layer of cheesecloth, leaving enough overhang to enclose the contents. Set aside.

Drain off any liquid from the cheese. Tip the cheese into a

bowl and beat it smooth. Gradually beat in the *crème fraîche*, and continue beating until the mixture thickens to fairly firm peaks. Spoon the mixture into the molds, tapping them gently on the work surface to settle their contents. Fold the overhanging cheesecloth over the top. Stand the molds on a trivet or rack so that the mixture can drain, and chill in the refrigerator or another cold place for at least 3 hours or overnight.

Unwrap the cheesecloth and turn out each cheese heart on to an individual plate. You can serve the Coeurs à la Crème just as they are, with a little sugar for those who wish it. Or you can pour over cream. They are also very good with seasonal fruits – soft, red fruits go particularly well – or a simple accompaniment of red currant or grape jelly, or honey.

## SERVING SUGGESTIONS

*small amount of sugar*

*½ cup light cream*

*seasonal fruit, either whole or puréed, or the honey, jelly or jam of your choice*

**Serves 2**

*Passion Fruit Salad*

# ACKNOWLEDGEMENTS

## AUTHOR'S ACKNOWLEDGEMENTS

First, I would like to thank Eleanor Lines and Simon Rigge for asking me to write this book. Next, I must express my deepest gratitude to Margaret Sweetnam, to whom this book is dedicated, for testing many of the recipes; and for helping, beyond the call of duty, with the cooking for the photographs. I must also say thank you to Pippa Normanton and Mrs. Peter Buchan for their most helpful contributions to the Test Kitchen.

! should also like to extend my warmest thanks to Jan Baldwin, who photographed this book, and to her assistant Brian Leonard, for their total dedication and professionalism. Thanks also go to David Seaton in whose flat the cover of the book was photographed. And I must send my best love to Timothy Fraser for making editorial meetings such a pleasure, and for being so patient when my copy was late.

I would like to record my special debt to Nigel Miskin, for undertaking miscellaneous research. And I owe a huge thank you to Anna Hall for her friendship and support while I wrote this book.

Finally, I would like to express my thanks to the staff at Wainwright & Daughter, and Curnick, both in Fulham Road, London; and also the marvellous staff at A.A. King, Kings Road, London.

## PICTURE CREDITS

The photographs in this book were taken by Jan Baldwin, assisted by Brian Leonard. The cover photograph was taken by Bob Komar. The artwork illustrations are by James Robins.

## OTHER ACKNOWLEDGEMENTS

The editors would like to thank: Valerie Chandler, Kathryn Cureton, Joanna Edwards, Katherine Judge, Alison Leach, Rob Mitchell, Christine Noble, Helen Seccombe, Nancy Webber.

# INDEX